To "Maura"
"an All-Star Nurse"
John Reardon

ALL-STAR
DADS

By JOHN REARDON

Published by Glacier Publishing
40 Oak Street
Southington, CT 06489
(860) 621-7644

Manufactured in the United States of America
ISBN 0-9650315-4-3
1. Parenting
2. Self-Help
3. Psychology

Edited, Design and Typesetting by Glacier Publishing
Cover Design by Josie Reardon

Printed & Bound in the United States of America

Other Books Available Through Glacier Publishing
Same Game, Different Name (0-9-650315-1-9)
Whalers Trivia Compendium (0-9-650315-0-0)
Forever Whalers (0-9-65315-3-5)

Table of Contents

A special message
from Mo Vaughn and his parents

Like most fathers, Leroy Vaughn smiled once he noticed his son enjoyed playing sports.

"Before you play baseball after school," Leroy would tell his son, "make sure your homework assignments are finished. Success in the classroom leads to success on the field."

Vaughn and his wife sensed their son had special skills, both in the classroom and on a baseball diamond. From the sandlots of Norwalk, Connecticut to the prep school fields at Trinity Pawling in New York, Mo Vaughn attracted the interest of scouts. The recruiters soon monitored his collegiate career at Seton Hall where the power-hitting first baseman emerged as one of the premier players in the country.

In 1989, the Boston Red Sox took Vaughn as the 23rd player on the first round. Within a couple of years, Vaughn established himself as one of the top players in the major leagues. A perennial All-Star, he was named MVP of the American League in 1995.

Away from the ballpark, Vaughn finds the time to work with youngsters throughout New England. He listens and advises future adults to establish goals and to stay in school.

"I owe everything to my parents," Vaughn says. "They have been positive and major influences on my life, long before I started hitting a baseball. Dad stressed the importance of education and not to take shortcuts. He suggested to set a goal and worked hard to reach it.

"My mom is the greatest. She told me every day 'to believe and you will achieve.' She is always upbeat and positive.

"I hope this book will be an inspiration to parents everywhere. It has been said many times that baseball is a game of confidence. I believe that. When a team is on a roll, everyone's spirit is up. You come to the ballpark believing you can overcome any situation.

"I feel the same way about parenting. Getting a child to think confident begins in the home. My parents are still my role models."

Dedication
In memory of my dad, John T. Reardon Sr.

Introduction

Changing the Way You Think

My dad was a tobacco farmer, Latin teacher and a lover of sports. For over 54 years he would ask his students to translate the following sentences from Latin:

"O sibili si ergo, fortibuses in ero.
Nobili demis trux sewatis enim?
Cowsendux!"

Today when I ask young fathers to do the same, they become totally confused and unable to do it. In order to understand my dad's humor I then ask you to also consider the following quote:

"If you always think the way you always thought,
you'll always get what you always got."

The students, as well as the fathers, do not see the joke in the Latin quote until it is pointed out to them. The quote should be read phonetically, in English, as: "O see Billy see her go forty buses in a row, no Billy them is trucks so what's in 'em? Cows and ducks!" At this point I'd like to repeat:

"If you always think the way you always thought,
you'll always get what you always got."

The same holds true for parenting. This book will help you to change your way of thinking about parenting. Once you begin to practice the techniques suggested, you may notice a difference in your child's behavior. You also may sense a stronger bond of family, a foundation based on respect and self-control, not only for today's ever-changing society but a model for tomorrow's parents.

Chapter I
Pre-Game Notes

Dad, You Are Important

When parents decide to attend a parenting workshop, they commit the time because they want to help someone they love.

Raising children isn't easy. Think back for a moment and ask yourself who played a pivotal role in your development?

Many people respond by saying "dad."

It's a good try but not correct.

The person most important in **your** development is **you**.

You are important, more important than you realize.

This may come as a shocker because our culture trains parents, especially fathers, to be a "Super Dad." You have seen him in action. He's the problem solver with an ingrained belief to take responsibility for everything and thus do everything humanly possible to make life easier for his children.

Society has done a masterful sales job on pitching this image. Look at the daily messages sent from advertisers, the ones which coax you to supply your children with the latest toy, or the tastiest fast-food meal.

The more you examine what is being suggested, the more the job of "Super Dad" seems to be one of being a "go-fer." Go get everything and give it to your children.

And should you fail to supply what is projected to be happiness for your children, you are prone to manipulation.

You know the routine.

It has happened in a department store or the supermarket.

"Dad," the youngster says, "I want a toy."

"No," you say, annoyed at first yet determined to advance the shopping cart and avoid a long line at the checkout counter.

Undaunted, the youngster tries again. This time, there are some common manners in the approach.

"May I please have that toy," the youngster says.

"No," you say, a bit more authoritative with a tad of redness forming on the skin of your neck.

The youngster begins to sulk. The stage is now set.

"I know mom would have bought it for me," the youngster says.

You rub your hands on your forehead. You try to reason with your child.

"Look at me," you say. "Do I look like mom?"

The child, still not convinced, retorts with another comparison.

"Jimmy's dad bought one for him. Dad, I really want one. Please."

In desperation, you pull out your wallet. You open it.

"Look here. I don't have the cash."

The youngster, still determined to win the showdown, notices a credit card.

"What about the plastic money?"

The kid smiles. He also sees dad smiling.

The child knows he's won. Another "A" in hassling.

In essence, the youngster has learned that all "no" means is "yes" later. Learn how to hassle the old man. The more you hassle him, the odds weigh in favor of getting what you want.

Well, dad. What do **YOU** want?

Do you want to endure more situations like this?

Would you like a means to defuse situations like this?

Besides saving a few dollars and adding more gray hairs, there is a way.

Answer this question.

Who is the most important person in the world?

Think about it.

Who is the most important person in the world?

Before you say the president, the pope or Michael Jordan, maybe you should look in the mirror.

The person reflecting back at you is the most important person in the universe.

Don't be shocked.

Most dads are. It takes time to realize it and to reinforce it.

Once you do, not only will you see yourself in different terms but you also will be doing an incredible favor for your family. The concepts about decision-making and taking responsibility will shift to the shoulders of those who will be held accountable.

Here's another way to look at it.

Ask yourself this question.

Who is the only one guaranteed to be at your funeral?

Don't be startled by this one.

You'll probably say "my wife and kids."

You might be right.

But there is only **one person** guaranteed to be at your funeral.

It's the same person you see every day in the mirror.

Believe in Yourself

Brett Butler plays outfield for the Los Angeles Dodgers. He was diagnosed with cancer of the tonsils in 1996. He was given only a 70 percent chance of survival.

Much like the determined player he is on the playing field, Butler not only overcame cancer but made it back to the lineup before an injury prematurely ended his season.

How did Butler battle both disease and skeptics?

"If you don't believe in yourself, nobody else will," he says. "That's something my dad told his children all the time. Don't let anybody tell you that you can't do it."

Besides prayer, Butler recalled his dad's philosophy often during his recovery and comeback.

"When children see that we consider ourselves important, you have constructed a model for them to follow," he says. "They see themselves as important and significant. They begin to understand the responsibility involved in taking care of the most important person in the world."

A Pleasant Morning

The sun may not shine every day but if you start the day with a little sunshine, the positive glow will emerge as a strong cue for children.

The smile is critical. Research shows that the most important part of a relationship will occur in the first seven seconds. When we meet a new person, judgments are instantaneous. A smile can make all the difference.

That's why I greet all the children outside the main school entrance with a smile as they arrive for the day. I often begin each morning with a riddle as well. I try to relax the children so they can have fun learning the day's lessons. If I can show them I am happy and the teaching staff is happy, we have established a successful environment for education.

A smile and a pleasant "Good morning" do make a difference. That is the philosophy which Japanese author Reiko Uchida offers in her book <u>Journey into the Twenty-first Century.</u>

I trace my smile back to Europe. My four grandparents came to the United States with the same dreams of all immigrants. A chance for a better life. That's why I often say I have an FBI background. The FBI stands for Foreign Born Irish.

"Top 'o the morning to you," I'll say as a daily greeting.

"And the rest of the day to yourself," will be the reply.

Setting Goals

Grandmother kept a diary. So did my dad. I have kept one, too.

The chronicles have helped members of my family realize how important we are and what we must do.

There's an entry in my grandmother's book for May 29, 1911 where her husband, my grandfather, stepped on a chicken bone in the yard at the family tobacco farm in Windsor, Connecticut.

The incident happened on a Monday. Gramps tried to seek medical assistance but the country doctor was not home to attend to the wound.

By Thursday, Gramps finally received help but it was too late. Within three days, he couldn't swallow. His jaw had locked up. My grandmother knew her husband was dying. She summoned Father Kane to anoint the man she loved.

The convulsions began within a week. On Wednesday, there were 27 before midnight. The next one came at 12:15 a.m. on Thursday. A couple of short ones followed. The last one proved fatal that June morning in 1911.

Grandma Reardon was on her own to raise five children, the youngest being five years old.

Throughout the diary, there are short entries like "Poor Papa, gone 25 days" or "Poor Papa, gone 25 months" or "Poor Papa, gone 25 years." There are also comments about how she raised her children and ran the farm by herself. She believed in a rearing philosophy called "old fashioned horse sense" based on how a mare takes care of her young foals.

The youngest child was my father. He worked many a summer in the fields. He eventually became a Latin teacher, working over five decades in education.

I still have a coin that my dad found one day. While plowing the fields, Ben Franklin, the family horse, all of a sudden stopped. My dad soon knew why. The horse had sensed there was something in the soil. It was a silver piece from the 1800s.

Grandma faithfully made notes in her diary. She recorded the day's events and also included what positive plans she had for another person the next day. This was something the more famous Ben Franklin had suggested a century earlier.

Father in Community

There's an African proverb which says "it takes a village to raise a child." It holds true in every culture.

In a community, there is a world of family, role models and caretakers, from neighbors to a place of worship.

Robert Simon, a social worker and educator, says he learned to be an ambassador from the parish pastor.

In athletics, he learned to be a coach by watching the mentors he had as a youth.

In the kitchen, his ability to prepare a meal was mastered by helping his mother.

Simon credits his love of education to a feisty grammar school teacher who refused to take "no" for an answer as much as his strength in communication to a scholastic social studies instructor who sought responses to questions formulated like an oral essay.

"These many lessons," Simon says, "are why the village needs to be maintained. If any of us are to begin to achieve our true capabilities, we must have them nurtured, beginning at an early age and continuing throughout our lives. Important lessons in life can be learned or taught by anyone. The goal is to give a youngster guidance through positive characteristics.

"My father was a salesman. Because he was on the road so much, my grandfather filled in the gaps. Grandpa taught me to work with my hands. He taught me why it's important to be organized.

"Grandpa ran a neighborhood grocery store. He also owned a couple of houses and an apartment building which he rented and maintained. One summer day, I guess I was about 10 years old, he handed me a nail apron and a hammer and said, 'Let's go to work.'

"I didn't realize it at the time, but it was an apprenticeship in practical education. If I had asked grandpa where we were going, he could have said, 'We're going to a place where you can start learning how to be a confident and self-reliant man.' And he would have been exactly right."

Lilly's Loose
(by Sue Pettit)

Lilly is the operator
at the switchboard of my brain.
> *And when she starts reacting,*
> *my life becomes insane.*
She's supposed to be employed by me
and play a passive role
> *But - anytime I'm insecure, -*
> *Lilly takes control.*

Lilly's loose, Lilly's loose,
Lilly's loose today!
> *Tell everyone around me*
> *just to clear out of my way.*
The things I say won't make much sense,

ALL-STAR DADS

all **COMMON SENSE** is lost
 `Cause when Lilly's at the switchboard,
 my wires get crossed.

Lilly is my own creation,
thought I needed her with me
 To organize and then recall
 all my life's history.
But she started taking liberty
with all my information
 And wherever she starts plugging in,
 I gets a bad sensation.

Lilly's loose, Lilly's loose,
Lilly's loose today.
 Tell the world to hurry by
 and stay out of my way.
I'm feeling very scattered.
I'm lost in my emotion.
 Lilly's on a rampage
 and she's causing a commotion.

She looks out through my eyeballs
and sees what I do see,
 Then hooks up wires to my past -
 and thinks she's helping me.
When I'm in a good mood,
I can smile at her endeavor.
 But when I'm in a bad mood,
 Lilly's boss... and is she clever.

Lilly's loose, Lilly's loose,
Lilly's loose today.
 Tell all my friends and relatives
 to stay out of the way.
I don't give hugs and kisses
when I'm in this frame of mind.
 And please don't take me seriously.
 It'd be a waste of time.1

A Nickel's Worth

People spend a fortune in therapy to help their children.

One family I know spent over $100,000 to assist a son.

Another used only a nickel to photocopy a poem called "*Lilly's Loose*" and the relationship between a father and his son improved dramatically.

When the two became too upset to reason, they walked to the refrigerator and read the poem affixed to the door by "I Love You" magnets.

No person has a right to control your emotions.

That job is yours.

And you must do the job.

If you don't, no one else will.

Handle With Humor

Dads who learn to control Lilly realize how important it is to see the humor in situations in raising their children. I know my dad needed these skills when I was young.

At age two, my parents and I were living in a three-story apartment when I locked myself in the bathroom on the third floor. The only way my folks could get me out was using a three-section ladder from the East Windsor Fire Department.

When the firemen climbed through the window and forced the door open to rescue me, I pointed to the bathroom door and began using short answers. I told my dad, "Grant fix." It was in reference to Mr. Grant, the owner of the house.

A year later my dad was challenged to see the humor when we were driving on Main Street in South Windsor and I asked him what purpose a certain handle in the truck had. Before dad could tell me, I had pulled the lever which put the vehicle's dumping mechanism in action. There we were, in the center of town, with a full load of potatoes all over the street.

ALL-STAR DADS

My dad's ultimate challenge to see humor came from baseball. My father had obtained an autographed baseball of his favorite team, a memento that featured the signatures of Lefty Grove, Jimmy Foxx and Mickey Cochrane of the 1929 Philadelphia A's. Dad often reminded me never to use the special baseball because it had writing on it. One summer day I had misplaced my old, black-taped baseball. A neighborhood game had to be played so I took my dad's treasured one. With an ink eraser, I cleaned the ball of pen marks. I dashed out of the house, telling my friends, "I found a ball. We bat first."

Years pass. Grandpa sits back and smiles as Julie, my then two-year-old daughter, decorates the bathroom with toilet paper and says, "Daddy fix."

A second adventure happened at Disney World when Susan, my other daughter, went exploring to find Mickey Mouse. Upon finding her and about to read the riot act, she smiled and said "Hi, daddy." Short answers often sum up a situation.

Grandpa's greatest smile came when doctors, who were about to operate on my son John for a nasal problem, phoned the family with a message. As the surgeons prepared for the procedure, they uncovered a tiny ball of twine my youngster had stored in his nose for future use.

These incidents suggest humor can deflate almost any situation. We need to laugh. We need to love. That's amplified in *It Could Have Been Funny*[1]:

It Could Have Been Funny
(by Sue Pettit)

It could have been funny - what happened last night.
It could have been funny - she looked quite a sight.
When a Halloween "glow stick"
popped open and dribbled,
its contents of green glow upon her did scribble.

It could have been funny.
We could have all laughed.
But I was too tired
and my good mood had passed.

As I stared with chagrin at the mess she had made,
I knew I'd explode if around her I stayed.
So instead of some laughter, sweet moments to share,
I got mad and I left her with a cold, scolding stare.

Now the mess is cleaned up
*   and my tiredness is gone*
And I "see" a new sight
*   in the new morning dawn.*

How different, how pleasant, how fun it would be
To turn back the clock in this mood I would see
The child that I love
GLOWING GREEN *in the night.*
And I'd laugh with her, sharing her startled delight.
Then we'd wash it all off and she'd climb into bed
And I'd tuck her in gently and kiss her forehead.

Yes, it could have been funny
Now it's clear to me!
My moods really "change"
What I feel, what I see.

As a dad learns to manage anger, he masters a skill to refrain from yelling at his children. You realize you often become angry when tired.

Give yourself space and time to relax before speaking. Think of *Lilly's Loose* as a way to delay acting on anger. Work at talking yourself through situations before taking it out on your children.

And dad, remember **YOU** are the most important person in the world.

The focus here is learning to relax. Stay focused while battling fatigue. It can be done.

Remember the times fishing at the lake and how happy you were when a rainbow trout fought hard and swallowed more of the hook?

Recall the feeling when you used the net to bag the catch of the day?

Use this analogy to unhook yourself from anger. The more you struggle, the more the anger will 'hook' you.

Another way to look at it might be to focus on the body language that a hitter employs before entering the batter's box.

From the moment he exits the on-deck circle until the one-on-one confrontation with the pitcher begins, a hitter must find a comfort zone. An observer may notice a couple of practice swings as part of the preparation process or the distance a hitter may station himself near home plate, but in the mind, it's up to the batter to visualize a snapshot of relaxation. He must be totally focused on the path of the baseball and thinking "hit." Distractions, like noise from the spectators or comments from opposing players, must be blotted out.

The hitter must stay in control. . . just like a dad.

You must practice techniques to offset anger just like a hitter works at improving his eye with more batting practice.

Learn to recognize the times when you are "bugged" by your children. Prepare yourself with strategies and keep your sense of humor. You and your children will grow.

On the highway, we have all found ourselves in a situation where a motorist has not used a signal light to turn or showed little courtesy at an intersection.

It takes skill to control anger.

It takes practice.

It takes courage.

It is easier to exceed the speed limit than it is to drive within the law.

It is easier to yell at your children than to use delayed consequences and short answers.

Dads, you can achieve patience but it is hard work..

Remember what was suggested a few pages earlier?

**"If you always think the way you always thought,
you'll always get what you always got."**

There are so many preconceived ideas which can stop us from becoming better dads.

We have to remember the poem *"Lilly's Loose"* and not become upset when things do not go our way.

We have to remember to keep our humor. The following story suggests how we can change the way we think.

The FBI

When we think of the FBI, we usually think of the Federal Bureau of Investigation. But for me, it is a reminder that I am from Foreign-Born Irish grandparents who had a great belief in the same values as Billy Martin, General Patton, and other great drill sergeants. For my wife, FBI means a Foreign-Born Italian parent. If her dad said to do something, she did it.

At a parenting workshop, a father told me he was also FBI, Foreign-Born Iranian! His grandparents also had a strong belief in drill sergeant mentality.

The concept of a drill sergeant has proven workable for the short term in baseball. In the military, it is a way of life. In cultures where there was a great deal of community support from the extended family, a parental drill sergeant had an impact upon the family structure.

But with today's ever-changing society, it just doesn't work.

Thomas and Patrick

Thomas was an old Irish bartender in South Boston. Patrick, a new customer, approached him and ordered three beers. Patrick would then take a sip from each mug and enjoyed his evening in the pub. After a few visits, Thomas told the new regular he could order one beer at a time and he might enjoy more of them. Patrick preferred to drink his way and told Thomas a story.

When he had left Ireland with his two brothers, the sons promised their mother that they would always stay together. As time passed, one brother decided to settle in Germany. Another went to Vancouver. Patrick, meanwhile, kept the family together in spirit, drinking one beer for the brother in Germany, a second for his brother in the Canadian Pacific and one for himself.

After a few months of the same routine, Patrick entered the bar and asked for only two beers. Thomas, the bartender, was a bit surprised. He wondered if something had happened to one of Patrick's brothers and asked if there had been a death in the family. Patrick began to chuckle. He appreciated Thomas's concern.

"Oh I'm still having my beers for my brother in Germany and in Canada," Patrick said. "I have given up beer for Lent."

The Last Burglary

A burglar had been keeping watch on a certain house in the neighborhood. Within a few days, after logging movements at the home, he sensed it was time to go to work.

It took handful of seconds for the thief to pick the door lock.

Playing it safe, he entered the house softly and asked, "Is anyone home?"

Seconds later, a small voice replied, "I am home and Jesus is watching you."

The burglar, a tad fearful, pulled out his flashlight.

Again he asked, "Is anyone home?"

The voice announced, "I am home and Jesus is watching you."

The burglar then used the flashlight to scan in the direction towards the voice. The thief breathed a sigh of relief when he realized it was a parrot in a cage.

Relaxed, the burglar moved forward with a stride of confidence . . . until his lantern zeroed in on a mouthful of teeth. The jaws belonged to a Doberman pinscher sitting below the bird.

"Jesus," the parrot said. "**Attack!**"

Jim Fay, a national educational consultant, tells two of his favorite stories. Both are based on actual situations.

The Pencil

When I was a high school administrator, a teacher had a problem with one of his math classes. A certain group of students in one section refused to bring writing instruments to class so the instructor had to supply the pupils with pencils. When class was dismissed, the students either kept the pencils or had chewed off the erasers, leaving the graphite sticks virtually useless.

Miffed at the group's attitude, the teacher tried every method he knew to reach the students. He yelled. He screamed. There were detentions. Parental conferences. Nothing worked.

One day, he asked me to cover his class for a few minutes. He also instructed that I send one student, who was the group leader, to the men's room.

Within a minute, the student returned to class.

A short time later, the teacher was back.. A buzz soon went around the room.

"Thanks Jim," the teacher said who resumed his lecture on proofing triangles.

A couple of weeks went by and I noticed there were no more referrals from the teacher about the pencil dilemma. A month later, I asked him what had happened.

"You should have seen the look on his face," he said.

I cracked a smile when the teacher told me that when the class leader had entered the bathroom, he found the instructor opening up a box of pencils and washing the eraser ends in the toilet bowl.

"What are you doing?" the student asked.

"Oh, I only do this to the pencils I give out to students," he said.

Right in the Kisser

I had been called by an administrator of a Pacific Northwest junior high school to solve a problem where girls in the eighth grade were vandalizing school property with lipstick.

For several weeks, the principal had tried just about everything. There were class meetings. Detentions. Suspensions. The problem in the bathrooms only mounted.

When I arrived,I explained I had no idea as to how this problem could be solved. The principal took me for a tour of the school and our conversation was overheard by a new custodian.

"I think I can end the problem" she said. "When's recess?"

The morning break was due in about half hour.

"Send the girls in at that time," the custodian said.

Vandalism had been a concern since the girls, trying various shades of lipstick, would blot their lips on the mirrors and walls of the bathroom.

When the bell sounded for recess, several girls entered the restroom. What they saw resulted in the end of an era as the custodian, dipping a mop into the toilet bowl, was washing down the walls and mirrors.

"What's the matter?" the custodian asked. "This is the way I always clean the walls in here."

The girls stared at her aghast.

One upchucked in a corner.

Another passed out.

My stay on the coast was over. [2]

Teaching by Example

When my daughter Susan was younger, our family went to Florida for spring training one year and stayed in Winter Haven. My dad and I had always been fans of the Athletics, no matter if the team was located in Philadelphia, Kansas City, or Oakland. Living in Connecticut, we often enjoyed debates with our neighbors over which team was better, our A's or New England's beloved Boston Red Sox.

On this day, Susan and I were swimming in the hotel pool when Bill "Spaceman" Lee, a pitcher for the Bosox, entered the pool for a swim. Sue and I were playing catch and an errant toss landed near Lee. The lefty threw it back to my daughter.

We had taught Susan not to talk to strangers but I took exception this particular time and suggested she could have a catch with Bill.

When I mentioned he was on the Red Sox team, my daughter immediately got out of the water.

"I won't stay in the pool with any Red Sox," she said.

As dads, we have to remember that our children are great listeners but poor interpreters. Susan had learned prejudice against the Red Sox because of the many discussions I had with her grandfather. Dads have to remember that what they model is what their children will learn.

A Promise From The Rocket

Roger Clemens pitched briefly in the minor leagues and one of his early stops was with the New Britain Red Sox. At the time, a future teammate of the Rocketman, Al Nipper, was living at my dad's house.

The players often talked with ballpark help. Some of the toughest jobs are in the kitchen. My daughter, who worked in the concession stand at Beehive Field, always preferred fast ballgames because that meant a shorter shift and an opportunity to get home earlier.

One afternoon in late August, Clemens and Nipper saw Sue before the game. The pitchers, between bites on hotdogs, vowed today's game would be quick.

"No problem tonight," Nipper said.

"That's right," Clemens said. "Joe Buzas will be the only person complaining. The strong box will be lighter tonight."

Buzas, who owned the ballclub, amassed a good fortune through concession and souvenir sales from the ballpark. Like any baseball promoter, Buzas preferred longer games, ones where opposing pitchers believed the strike zone was high and outside.

"Al," Sue asked. "Are you going to keep your promise?"

"Certainly," Nipper said. "Roger's pitching."

Everyone laughed.

"Sue," Clemens said, "this one's for you."

That night, Clemens kept his promise to my daughter and also gave baseball fans a look into the future when he rang up the strikeouts. Clemens literally took the bats out the hands of the Reading Phillies. The ballgame was over in 1:41 and my daughter was able to go to a movie with friends.

Superior talent and a commitment to hard work makes for a super athlete but don't overlook what little challenges can do for motivation.

Some children need extra encouragement to stay motivated. Dads don't have to make promises but a few minutes every day with a child to help to solve a math problem or to improve the grammar in a writing assignment supplies assurance to a youngster.

Eck's Home Video

Dennis Eckersely has chalked up plenty of saves out of the bullpen over the years. Maybe his biggest "save" happened away from the ballpark.

Troubled by an addiction to alcohol, Eckersley's baseball career was in jeopardy. So was his life.

One day, his sister-in-law suggested he view a movie. She put it in the VCR and it proved to be a real eye-opener. The person in the film under the influence of alcohol. His behavior, in a word, was embarrassing.

The shock of seeing himself in an altered state was the first step in recovery for Eckersley. He overcame his addiction to alcohol, regained a love for life and revived his sagging career on the diamond.

That's one reason why I explain to teachers to keep a small mirror on their desks. It's there to get a look at themselves if they feel they have a problem or "*Lilly is loose.*" The reflection in the mirror is the same one the students in the classroom see.

Polly, Is That Me?

Reiko Uchida,[3] a Japanese parenting expert, tells of a lesson she learned from her pet.

One day she returned from shopping and she listened as a parrot called out the name of her oldest child in an unpleasant voice.

Upon hearing the tone in the words, Reiko knew the voice would bother anyone.

The parrot spoke again. This time, the words were soft and loving as the bird called out the name of her youngest daughter.

Reiko immediately realized that the parrot was merely imitating her. The pet had spoken in the same voice she used when calling her children.

The incident did more than shock Reiko. It changed her behavior and mended family relations.

---

[1] "Lilly's Loose" and "It Could Have Been Funny" are from Coming Home, a collection of poems by Sue Pettit and vailable from:
   Sunrise Press, P.O. Box 788, Fair Oaks, CA 95628 (800) 456-7770

[2] For more information on Jim Fay's work and his short answers contact:
   Cline Fay Institute, 2207 Jackson Street, Golden, CO 80401 (800) 338-4065

[3] Reiko Uchida may be reached at: 98 Betsuhori, Odawana,
   Kanagawa-Ken, 250-02 Japan

Chapter 2
A Single To Center

A New Way of Thinking

Dads who keep a sense of humor can also make a major breakthrough in parenting by remembering *"Lilly's Loose"* when situations arise in the home. Once you become familiar with the following lists, you can defuse virtually every situation as your children learn more about responsibility.

The first list illustrates how children plot to manipulate parents with strategies designed to gain power and attention. Dads need to realize when they fall into the hassling trap.

Debate with a child and you are no longer the figure of authority.

In essence, you have lost control of a situation.

Think for a moment and recall a recent debate with a person who has emptied a couple of six packs.

Feel like you wasted words and time since someone under the influence of alcohol "knows" he's right and is an expert on any subject.

Why create a hassle for yourself?

Why not use better judgment? You cannon reason with a person in that state of mind.

Take a few minutes to realize how easily your children have mastered the skills on the first list called "**A Child's Garden of Diversion.**"

Examine the list.

Dad, are you able to realize how your children try to gain your attention? Once you realize they are using skills to manipulate you, it's vital to employ short responses to improve your parenting technique.

Jim Fay's list of **"Short Answers"** as suggested in his book Parenting with Love and Logic will help defuse many situations.

When you are relaxed, you don't rush to solve problems. You delay consequences. You don't lose your temper.

When you supply short answers to children, you offer a gift of time to yourself and the first checkpoint to becoming a better father.

A Child's Garden of Diversions
(quotes you have heard)

1. "You like Tommy better than me"
   (partiality to siblings)

2. "But you <u>told</u> me to . . ."
   (faking compliance)

3. "You can't do that. I'll call Child Protective Services."
   (against the Constitution)

4. "You won't believe this, but . . . "
   (the tall tale)

5. "It was only a <u>little</u> scratch"
   (making big mistakes look small)

6. "Mommy said I could."
   (parental division)

7. "Joey's parents let him."
   (affirming the excellence of other families)

8. "I saw Tommy doing something much worse than I did."
   (attempting diversion)

9. "Don't you think I'm capable of ..."
   (disavowing trust)

10. "You can do what you want to me. I don't care."
    (disavowing parental concern)

11. "It's not my fault. If Jimmy hadn't . . . "
    (putting the blame on others)

Jim Fay's Short Answers

Probably so.
I know.
Nice try.
I bet it feels that way.
What do you think you're going to do?
I don't know. What do you think?
Bummer. How sad.
Thanks for sharing that.
Don't worry about it now.
That's an option.
I bet that's true.
Maybe you'll like what we have for the next meal better.
What do you think I think about that?
I'm not sure how to react to that. I'll have to get back to you on it.
I'll let you know what will work for me.
I'll love you wherever you live.

Be the judge the next time a hassle comes along.

It's important to be careful with your response. It should be said with empathy and love. Not sarcasm.

In a short time, you will reap a bounty. So will your children.

When you choose an appropriate answer, you begin to maintain control over a situation.

Remember. Regardless of which short answer you select, use it until the child accepts.

Here's an example.

Two brothers are fighting. Both try to have dad blame the other brother for the altercation.

"Dad, Tommy hit me first," Jimmy says.

"No Dad. Jimmy hit me first," Tommy says.

Instead of becoming embroiled in the argument, why not say, "Bummer. How sad."

By such a response, dad has remained neutral. He has acknowledged his sons, but removed himself from the argument.

Should the hassle continue, it might be necessary for dad to repeat the phrases until the youngsters get tired of trying to hassle you.

In a matter of seconds, peace is restored. It's likely both boys will end up going outside and playing together.

Play Your Best Cards

Bill Gullickson pitched for several teams in North America. He also threw strikes for baseball teams in Japan. His approach to emotional control is simple.

"No matter the cards you're dealt," he says, "you must play them to best of your ability. No matter what you tell your kids to do and how to act, they are going to see how **YOU** act and copy it. You are the leader. So take the leading role."

A baseball team is only as strong as its leader.

So is a family.

Demands on time multiply daily in the workplace. Modern life is so fast, the pace can leave anyone frustrated, irritated and flustered.

A cup breaks during supper.

Juice is spilt on the rug in the family room.

Each mishap can trigger an explosion.

Words, often in rage, come spewing out like hot lava from an island volcano.

We have all broken a dish or spilt a drink.

Can you hear the echo of a voice that made your ears turn red.

Did you feel unloved, hurt and angry?

Did you ever say to yourself, "When I'm a parent, I will never say anything like that to my child."

How about it, Dad.

Have you kept your promise?

Children seek our attention. They want our love.

They also need to learn the consequences for making poor choices.

And dads, control your emotions.

We know the world is more complicated for adults. Just imagine what a jungle it can be for a youngster.

A little kindness and love starts each day with happiness.

Maybe you will see yourself in the following routine.

It's 6:30 a.m. The alarm clock rings. The day begins for you to get ready for work and for the children to get ready for school.

Do you hear yourself say. . .

Get out of bed.

NOW.

I told you to get up before.

You're not dressed yet?

Why isn't your bed made?

Get back in there and wash your face.

Brush your teeth.

Those clothes don't match.

That outfit is worse than the other one.

No child of mine will go to school dressed like that.

(Minutes later, at the breakfast table, the scene continues.)

I prepared breakfast.

Eat all of it.

Don't you know there are children starving in other parts of the world?

Put the dishes in the sink.

Better brush your teeth.

Get your jacket.

You don't make $15 million a year to wear your baseball cap backwards.

(The scene now shifts to the bus stop.)

Stop fighting while you wait for the bus.

Don't push getting on the bus.

Stay in line.

Keep your coat on.

(Now, it's 8:45 a.m. School begins and so has work.)

The youngster, whose had his self-image badly bruised, struggles to communicate with others.

At work, Dad gets a call from the principal. He learns his son was involved in a fight with another student and will be suspended for a week.

Dad, do you think life might be better if the morning ritual could be hassle free?

It can be.

It's up to you.

A Fox's Advice

A writer named Bob Fox recalls going to a baseball game with his dad at Crosley Field, a ballpark in Cincinnati which served as the home of the Reds for many years. On the ride home, the two shared a conversation which drifted from baseball into business.

Both father and son believe there is a chemistry associated with winning teams, much deeper than the smiles that follow a pennant

---

He is Just a Little Boy
by Bob Fox

He stands at the plate with his heart pounding fast.
The bases are loaded, the die has been cast.
Mom and Dad cannot help him, he stands all alone.
A hit at this moment, would send the team home.

The ball meets the plate, he swings and he misses.
There's a groan from the crowd, with some boos and hisses.
A thoughtless voice cries, "strike out the bum."
Tears fill his eyes, the game's no longer fun.

Do open you heart and give him a break.
For it's moments like this, a man you can make.
Please keep this in mind, when you hear someone forget.
He is just a little boy, and not a man yet.[4]

---

victory. A "family" might be too strong a word but if people are happy, it's an environment worth taking a second look at.

"Regardless of what you do later in life," Fox says, "you need to examine your heart. You want to beat the competition, but you want to do right by people. You must care about people as much as you care about profit. In the end, the two lead to success."

Today, at 85, Bob still has a strong love of baseball. His poem "*He is Just a Little Boy*" carries an eternal message to dads and coaches. A careless word can damage a child.

Dinner with the Boss

Dads, understand one thing. You possess skills beyond belief.

If we would think of our children as if they were the boss who came to dinner, would we talk to Mr. Brown in the same manner we talk to our children?

Mr. Brown, don't you know you have to eat your broccoli?

Mr. Brown, how could you spill your drink?

**If you always think what you always thought,
you will always get what you always got.**

A window gets broken.

Are the first words out of your mouth "Is anyone hurt?" or "Which one of you morons threw the ball?"

Seconds later, the telephone rings.

It's a college buddy on the line, someone you have not heard from in years.

Immediately, your mood and tone of voice change. You become a different person.

Dad, a window can always get fixed.

Recall the many gifts you received at Christmas and you wanted the holiday season to go on forever?

All you said was: "Dad, is that all?"

Remember dad getting angry.

"Don't you appreciate everything I've done for you?"

Did the same events occur this past holiday in your home?

An excited six-year old isn't equipped with the ability to say, "Christmas is great. I want it to go on forever."

Word choice is so critical. Remember that. Slow down. Remember not to let "*Lilly Loose*."

Common sense does make sense.

Stay on Course

Leaders are born every day and the strongest cues for guidance must come from the home on a daily basis. Such was the framework for Dick Balderson who recalls when his code of living was established.

"Dad showed us a model of respect, discipline and honesty," says the vice-president of the Colorado Rockies. "One way to teach people responsibility is through direction and consequences. You have to make yourself available, to direct and consult daily. Don't underestimate the value of feedback."

Balderson's office door is open for his employees. So was his dad's. In the home, Balderson says it's best to set realistic goals in connection with a child's age and ability.

"With a reachable target, kids can accomplish just about anything," he says. "But they need to be nurtured. . . with communication and with patience."

According to Balderson, here are the key steps for a new dad to be successful:

1. Marry a good woman
2. Want children
3. Communicate
4. Set goals
5. Reduce emotions and get into the "slow lane"
6. Prepare for bombs

Live Your Dream

Dreams don't often come true but one did for Ricky Bottalico, the ace relief pitcher of the Philadelphia Phillies.

Blessed with a strong arm, Bottalico found himself as a backup catcher early in his collegiate career.

"I had the dream of playing major league baseball and the confidence of reinforcement from my dad," he says. "It's amazing how the two are related."

All Bottalico had to do was find the right position. That occurred during his final years at Central Connecticut State when the coach ran short of pitchers.

"I could have quit baseball," Bottalico says. "My dad was a rock. He harped on my work habits and believing in yourself. I never stopped working to make my dream come true."

Sometimes fathers don't realize how their positive support can change the life of a young person.

Mastering a Lesson

Coaches are often "father figures" and George Redman never forgot a lesson during his scholastic career involving self-control.

A feisty and gritty performer, Redman was at his best playing football and baseball. In basketball, as a key reserve, he was often the first player off the bench.

"One year," he recalls, "my temper got the best of me. I wound up in a fight. And I paid the price."

His Bristol (Connecticut) High School coach had a rule about fighting. "One altercation," Redman recalls, "and you were assigned to the junior varsity team for three games. And you were the last one off the bench. Talk about being humbled."

The punishment worked. Besides getting teased by his peers, Redman, who went on to coach baseball at the collegiate level, gained valuable advice on self-discipline. "Mistakes are the biggest teacher," Redman says. "That was the best lesson I ever learned."

If a child can assist in setting the punishment beforehand, it is much more effective. A young person can accept a punishment more easily when he or she knows ahead of time what the penalty will be.

Inseams and Pigskins

An early season storm left the roads icy, so much that any motorist would have extreme difficulty keeping a car from skidding out of control.

And staying in control, especially tempering emotions, is often the toughest battle all dads encounter.

On the ride to school, dad knew the only passenger in the vehicle would be late for his fourth-grade class.

About a mile from school, the son remembered something.

"Dad, we have to turn back," he said. "I forgot to bring my football. I need it for recess."

Tears soon flowed.

Dad, who was doing his best to keep the family station wagon on the road, did his best to stay cool.

"So sad" and "nice try" were his responses.

The son, however, kept sobbing and pleading.

"Dad, can we go back?" the boy asked.

"Son," dad replied, "if you forgot your pants, I might think about going back."

The child began to laugh.

So did his dad.

As the car pulled into the school parking lot, the pair had one more exchange.

"Son," dad said, "have a good day in school."

"Dad," the boy said, "I love you."

When you change a mood by using humor you can turn a situation around. You have also kept "*Lilly Loose*" under control.

Book Confetti

As an avid reader, I think one of the most popular places to go with your youngster is the library. The weekly trips can be special. They also can take a different twist.

When a young boy decided to see what a pair of scissors could do to a borrowed book, "*Lilly*" was completely loose in Dad's mind.

Dad began to yell and scream.

The child, not impressed, stayed calm.

"Dad," he said, "it was just a book. There's a million more down at the library."

Not a bad line from a six-year old.

Stumped, dad had to find a way to solve this dilemma. A $5 book could easily be replaced. There was no price, he thought, on a lifetime message involving responsibility.

During a break at work, dad sought assistance.

"That happened to me," a colleague said. "Call the library. Maybe your son can work a couple of hours there to compensate for the book. He'll appreciate the printed word a little more. I know it worked for me."

Dad telephoned the library during lunch. He found an understanding voice and also a solution. It was decided that Junior would help the librarian every recess for a couple of weeks to cover the expense. Besides putting returned books in their proper places on the shelves, the experience opened a new world to the youngster.

"Dad, can you take me to the Public Library on Saturday?" the boy asked. "There are a couple of books I want to take out. I want to show you I can read them."

A situation which could have been a bad experience turned into a lesson in learning responsibility. A child needs to be taught that he has responsibility for his own actions.

Bobby and Blue

Both came from different backgrounds. Each enjoyed success on different coasts of the United States, reaching all-star status a number of times in their careers.

For Bobby Richardson, it was his dad who taught him how to live a good life based on attending church, reading God's words and praying.

For Vida Blue, it was making time to be with his children.

Few may have duplicated Richardson's table-setting ways for the New York Yankees in the 1960's or Blue's impressive pitching for the Oakland A's of the early 1970's. However, the world would be a better place if we followed Bobby's code of conduct and caring and Vida's strong feelings on parenting.

"Love, love and love your children." Blue says.

Like Father Like Son

Tom Grieve grew up in New England, in a home environment where he followed the lead of his father. A part-time outfielder for most of his seven seasons in the big leagues, Grieve has since spent over two decades in management, mostly with the Texas Rangers. He reflects on what traits his father amplified in his youth.

"We have to be accountable for our own actions and we need to stop blaming others or making excuses as a means of avoiding responsibility," Grieve says. "Kids watch every move we make. We are the model. It is unrealistic to expect a child to associate with high standards we set if we don't do the same ourselves. My father didn't teach me with words. It was his actions, the way he lived his life. Courteous and polite. He always treated people with respect, regardless of status. He's the one who instilled responsibility, about being honest and honorable. I've tried to develop those qualities."

Children learn by what they see. Dads who act the way they want their sons to act will eventually see results.

Respect at Any Age

In 11 seasons where his defensive skills outweighed offensive ones, Ray Berres never overlooked the moments his father shared with his children. He fashioned many of those traits into people skills, especially working with youngsters during a coaching career that spanned 20-plus years in the big leagues.

"I just turned 90," Berres says, "and I still try to emulate my father in every respect. Dad passed away when I was a youngster but I do remember his interest in his children in so many ways. He just wasn't 'Dad' in name only. He encouraged us. He was always there, to help us with our homework or have a catch in the backyard. That means so much. He made a point to read to us, to attend our activities, be it sports or a school play.

"It was my father's appreciation of others that set an ever-lasting foundation of discipline. The adage 'Do unto others as you would have them do unto you' was my father's motto. He showed me why encouragement, politeness and patience are essential to a great life."

A dad must be available to his child both emotionally and physically.

Foundation of Respect

If a batting coach offers guidance to struggling hitters, Mike Easler, one of the best in the business, proposes to employ the same techniques to help children accept responsibility.

"You need a foundation and some flexibility," he says. "That's something I learned from my parents. My dad was always there for his six sons and three daughters. That's how I learned about family values.

"I was fortunate to be teammates in Pittsburgh with Willie Stargell. Willie always talked about baseball being a game of mistakes. He said mistakes should be looked at as wonderful opportunities to grow.

"We often fail in life in trying to reach a goal. It's so important to stay on task, to work at getting better and make adjustments. You might want to be perfect, but do forgive yourself. Have patience. Keep anger away from your child.

"A hitter strives for consistency. Dad, do the same. Give your love to your children every day. Give them the first 10 minutes when you get home from work. You'll see the joy in their eyes. Love covers a million errors."

Easler's advice on hitting and parenting:

1. You need a foundation
    a. Hitting starts with the feet
    b. Parenting starts with the ten commandments
    c. You should model both
2. You need flexibility
    a. Hold the bat in a relaxed manner, bend at the knees
    b. Parenting - children learn to deal with friends and school
    c. Do it slowly
3. Find the gift which God gave you
    a. Easler found baseball
    b. Children respect God, parents, self and authority

c. Keep it simple on a solid foundation
4. Mistakes are wonderful opportunities to grow
   a. Baseball is a game of failure as Willie Stargell suggests
   b. We fail at times in life and we need to set a goal
   c. Become a consistent person
5.Dads give love each day
   a. Practice, practice
   b. Joy when dad arrives home
   c. Love covers a million errors
6. At bat in the game
   a. Remove the crowd
   b. Arriving at home, give the first 10 minutes to the family
   c. Stay on task

Every Day Challenges

Dale Murphy is rated among the better hitters during his 20-year career in the big leagues. What he remembers most about his introduction to the game were practice sessions in the backyard. He chased after whiffle golf balls that his father would hit.

"That helped me get a jump on a flyball," he says.

What also helped Murphy was the attitude his father instilled when he first started to play organized baseball.

"What sticks out is my first year," Murphy says. "I was eight years old. I think I had just one hit for the entire season. I never knew it wasn't very good. My dad never showed any concern about my lack of hitting. He wanted me to have fun.

"We have learned to be creative and realize a youngster can't do the job as well as we could. My kids make their beds. They were bumpy in the beginning. Not any more. Dad, it does get better."

Praising a child for job well done works wonders. Emphasize the positive aspects.

Dale and his wife believe as society has changed, so has the task to teach responsibility to children.

"It was easier to teach a child to be responsible when we lived on a farm. It just takes more time and planning to do it today," Dale says. "Parenting is the toughest job in the world. But it's also the most rewarding."

Gramps and Mrs. Smith

My father often did baseball research at the Hall of Fame library in Cooperstown, New York. Ken Smith was the curator at the Hall for many years. He always welcomed my dad.

After spending a week in the area a few years back, Mr. Smith invited our family to visit his home. It was like a miniature version of the Hall of Fame. Baseball pictures of Babe Ruth, Joe DiMaggio and many of the other greats adorned the walls of his den.

Following dessert, my wife, Josie, helped Mrs. Smith in the kitchen with the dishes. When it was time for coffee, Mrs. Smith asked her husband if he remembered the girl, a few years ago, who also went out of her way to help tidy up things after a dinner.

"Ken," she said. "Who was that girl? She was wonderful. A blonde girl. She came with Joe DiMaggio."

It was then we realized the girl was Marilyn Monroe.

If we always think with preconceived ideas, we often can miss reality.

Nice Guy After All

Clyde King was pitching one year for the Brooklyn Dodgers and his manager, Leo Durocher, was running short of arms. Durocher wondered if King could pitch out of turn in St. Louis.

"Leo had a way to convince anyone he could do something," King said. "Opponents remember Leo as a tough guy. He was. But he also had a way to boost a player's confidence. He believed in his players."

King volunteer to pitch. On an extremely hot day, King was exhausted but managed to go nine innings. The defense made the routine plays to support King and the Dodgers pulled out a win.

When the ballclub returned to Brooklyn, Durocher summoned King to his office. The manager wondered if a new sports coat hanging in the closet would fit the pitcher.

"It's too big for me," Durocher said. "Maybe it fits you."

"Oh, I don't know Leo," King said. "That jacket isn't in my league, you know."

"Clyde, will you please try the jacket on?"

King did. It seemed to fit as if it was made for him.

"Clyde," Durocher said. "I might as well get another one. That jacket fits you like you were measured for it. I'll have to order another one."

King was all smiles.

"Hey Leo. Thanks a lot."

The following day, a haberdasher from the neighborhood was in the clubhouse. He sought out King.

"How's the jacket fit?" he asked.

It was then the pitcher realized that Durocher had ordered the coat as a gift.

"Leo always said 'Nice guys finish last,' " King said. "Durocher was a nice guy."

Leadership Styles

From Leo Durocher to Billy Martin there have been baseball managers who have been known as "dictators." These managers want everything done their way or it's the highway.

As these men achieved success in sports, many fathers imitated them and attempted to raise their children in a dictatorial manner without love. Children raised in this environment will be well-behaved for the dad at first but soon will become resentful. They will retreat from their dad and look for ways of revenge. They will finally get even by acting in unacceptable ways.

These dads turn family life and sports into emotional abuse. Athletes who play a game they love under a dictatorial coach soon find that it spoils the game. Young men are quick to understand the non-logic of a drill sergeant philosophy which teaches the following: The more abuse you can give, the better off they will be. It's for their own good, the more they can take, the stronger they will become. Some dads have believed this. The results are devastating on children.

---

[4] Bob Fox may be reached at: P.O. Box 43, Brookville, OH 45309

A second leadership style developed during the Viet Nam era when helicopters rescued soldiers during combat missions were shown nightly on television newscasts.

Parents developed a similar technique to rescue their child whenever a mistake was made. They would fly into schools with forgotten lunches, musical instruments, homework, or whatever else the child did not bring.

Rather than have a child learn any responsibility or consequences, children raised in this manner where they never lost a toy or missed a lunch became shocked in adulthood when they had a car or house repossessed. Rescuing a child robs him of a learning experience.

Managers like Don Baylor, Dusty Baker, Walter Allston and Art Howe believe it is important to establish firm limits for players. They also have the ability to communicate with them as individuals. Dads must realize the secret of good communication in raising their children. Leo Durocher had this ability as he worked with a young pitcher named Clyde King.

Chapter 3
Ground-Rule Double

Bear Down

There are days when John Stupor sees a couple of pitchers on the Yale baseball team struggling with control.

"Bear down," he says. "Just bear down."

As a youngster, Stupor recalls hearing the same words from his father when the two had a catch in the backyard.

"Dad was never too tired to have a catch," he says. "I don't know how he did it. He worked in the coal mines and that wasn't easy.

"There were games later on where things got tough out there on the mound and I'd hear his voice, 'Bear Down' coming from the stands. Just knowing he was there and cared enough meant quite a lot to me.

"That's what I remember most about my father. He made the time and he was patient with us. Give time to your children. Be patient with them."

Lessons in Love

Confidence is related to attitude and Roy Smalley recalls the "loose herding" approach his father used in allowing his children to make choices for themselves.

"This old cowboy term makes a lot of sense," Smalley says. "It's important to establish rules where praise and discipline can be judged.

Just stick with quality values like integrity, responsibility and caring for others. Just be consistent in judgment.

"Once the ground rules are established, there is no need to harp, criticize, belittle or punish because the youngster knows what the consequences are if a rule is overlooked.

"The net result is you help your children become more responsible because they must learn to make decisions for themselves. It also helps a child's self-esteem because a confident child is a happy child."

Fathers should set firm ground rules for family values and make them clearly understood by the children.

Ice Cream Sundaes

Former big-league hurler Paul Giel, who returned to be athletic director at the University of Minnesota where he starred in football, remembers the summer day in his youth when he felt he was on top of the world.

"I had just pitched a no-hitter in a Little League game where I struck out a dozen batters," Giel says.

Upon his arrival home, the youngster raced up to his father who was working in the yard.

"How did your team do?" asked the boy's father.

"We won and I pitched a no-hitter."

"That's great."

Dad did his best not to criticize us. I didn't have to live through errors on the diamond like some kids but my dad's philosophy of encouragement didn't go unnoticed. I know my boys felt terrible about losing a ballgame. Once we pulled into the Dairy Queen for an ice cream, the mood usually changed.

Develop Your Talents

Sal Bando played 16 years in the big leagues. Today as an executive with the Milwaukee Brewers, Bando often reminds his coaches of the words his father often said.

"Let the player develop his own skills and talents," Bando says. "You can't press an athlete into something he can't be. Just because someone can run, it doesn't mean he can steal bases. Remember that when you are playing with your children. Don't press your son or daughter into something **YOU** want them to be.''

Dads should remember that each child is an individual, with different talents and abilities.

Heart Over Size

Bobby Shantz spent 16 years in the major leagues, a long tenure for someone who encountered many jokes about his frail 5-foot-6, 140-pound frame. The comments, however, stopped once he won 24 games in 1952 for the Philadelphia Athletics.

"I wouldn't give in to those big guys," Shantz says with a laugh. "In all honesty, the most important lesson in life is don't give up. That's something my father reminded me all the time.

"Today's dads have a tendency to be too forceful especially when it comes to Little League. There's too much emphasis on winning. Do your child a favor. Don't take the fun out of it. Let the youngsters enjoy the game, the opportunity to make friends and communicate with others. That's how you build confidence for a lifetime."

Honest Day's Work

Ron Guidry made his mark in baseball with the New York Yankees. Guidry won the Cy Young Award in the American League. He also won 20 or more games three times in his career.

As a youngster in Louisiana, Guidry took advantage of helpful comments from his father which served as an inspiration for his future success.

"The values of being honest and putting in a hard day's work can't be overlooked," Guidry says. "That's what my dad stressed to me. He also put an importance on respecting others. That's a good two-way street."

The Good Doctor

George "Doc" Medich made one of his biggest saves in 1978 before a scheduled game in Baltimore. During batting practice, a spectator was stricken. Medich, who was completing study in medicine, reacted quickly. He performed heart massage and revived the fan.

Being able to react to situations of any kind with confidence and composure, Medich says, date back to conversations with his father. Now a doctor in his native Pittsburgh, Medich had set goals, upon the urging of his family, to pursue a medical career once baseball ended.

"To reach any goal, you need support," Medich says. "I recall my dad was always there. He took an active interest in what I was doing. I know it made a difference. Just to see him in the stands or get a pat on the back after a game meant so much."

Buttons Are Forever

Clothing manufacturers have solved the mystery of losing buttons for parents. Most include an extra button on the inside of an item.

What happens if you lose a second button?

I found myself in that predicament a couple years ago. The thread that kept the bottom button attached to my winter jacket had come undone. I went the entire season shy a fastener. I prefer comfort over style. After all, it's only a button.

My wife noticed that my coat was not complete. So she decided to surprise me. She went shopping for a replacement button. Her travels resulted in a trip to the hospital.

Convinced she could find a button at a fabric store, my wife was so focused, she did not see a display platform clogging up an aisle. She tripped and broke her hip upon falling.

I started thinking about what occurred and it reinforced what I believe is true: "People do make a difference."

That's why I created a button pin which states "**I make a difference**" because every person is important.

I give these buttons to parents, teachers, students and visitors. I know how a button changed my life because someone wanted to help me.

There Are Rainbows

Jim Rice, a feared slugger many years for the Boston Red Sox, sat in the hospital. Tears filled his eyes. A nine-year old boy named Kyle Stanley was undergoing chemotherapy for a cancer. The child's father, a teammate of Rice's, sat in shock.

"Kyle's hero," Bob Stanley recalls, "was also mine. Jim helped me through a situation which I will never forget."

These days, Kyle has recovered and has become a golfer with promise for his scholastic team.

"You should see him hit the ball," Stanley says.

Stanley believes parents put too much pressure on their kids. "I don't recall my father ever raising his voice," Stanley says. "He was the most important person in my life. He put his family above everything."

Kyle's illness bonded Stanley's family as well as the Red Sox players. Baseball took a back seat for several months until the youngster recovered.

The strength of a child cannot be dismissed. A youngster can often be an inspiration for others.

Like Kyle, there was a student named Wade at our school who was sick with a form of leukemia. A new medical technique made it possible to save the boy's life. No question the youngster and his parents will face more challenges in the years ahead, but that family is closer and stronger to deal with each one.

Believe in rainbows because they are more than just symbols of hope. I recall the story about a father who loved playing with his children when his life was cut short, he told his boys and girls that he would send a rainbow so they would remember him.

We have seen rainbows twice.

When my father-in-law died, we saw a special rainbow and it filled our eyes with tears.

The second time was during the holiday season. We were separated from our daughter who is a physician. Julie, after working Christmas Eve, looked up towards the sky on Christmas morning.

She called us and was crying into the telephone. The sobs echoed happiness.

"Don't worry. I'm all right," she said. "And grandpa is with me. I just saw a rainbow."

Cupcakes and Open Ears

Carl Erskine rates among the better pitchers in the annals of the Brooklyn Dodgers, twice tossing no-hitters and once fanning 14 in a World Series game. He recalls throwing stones along the railroad tracks in Indiana to build up arm strength as well a daily catch with his dad in the backyard.

"My father was something," Erskine recalls. "He worked at the plant for General Motors and he always saved something from lunch. After a catch, he'd give me a cookie or a cupcake. I knew my dad was thinking about me each day and I never forgot that."

Erskine also never forgot what an opposing manager told him late one season in the minor leagues. "Jack Onslow came up to me and suggested I stop tipping off batters," Erskine says. "I had been hit pretty hard that day."

Erskine made the adjustments and was soon in the big leagues. "Someone was willing to help," Erskine says "and I was willing to listen. I'd say that's a pretty good formula for success."

Dads should be willing to seek mentors and learn from people who have had success in raising children. There is no stigma attached to not knowing the capital cities of countries around the world. But there is a problem if you decline to seek advice on how to raise your children.

A View From Space

Bill "Spaceman" Lee was one of the best left-handed pitchers in the history of the Boston Red Sox and maybe the franchise's most misunderstood philosopher.

When he saw the famed "Green Monster," Boston's most storied wall in left field at Fenway Park, for the first time, Lee asked "Do they leave it there during games?"

Lee was a competitive pitcher during his career. He credits his parents for his love for the outdoors and some of his beliefs.

"I often think back about the vacations to my grandfather's farm where we'd hunt and fish all day," Lee says.

It was during the Vietnam War when Lee began his pro baseball career and "left my Utopian dream and moved to a socialistic dream," he says.

"My dad grew up during the Great Depression and fought in World War II," Lee says. "He wondered every day when he was in the service if he would return to see his family. He believed in America. He also believed in hard work and love."

Lee shaped his values around what his father believed and "once I began asking questions," he says, "the more I found out that people don't always have answers that are best for society. Darwin's theory about survival of the fittest isn't practical. The technology is in place so everyone on the planet can share.

"As a dad today, I can model," Lee says. "But you can only lead a horse to water. I practiced for hours pitching a baseball and shooting a basketball, the same amount of time my son played Atari. Repetition is the answer for success. Kids who don't have this foundation don't learn sports. Dads who don't practice new ideas in parenting won't change their thinking."

A Twist of Apple Juice

Jay Johnstone had plenty of hits in his bat to last close to two decades in major league baseball. He also had the wit to get a laugh from everyone in the clubhouse.

One year at spring training in Vero Beach, Los Angeles manager Tommy Lasorda had been reminding his players about taking a required drug test. For some reason, Johnstone kept ducking the issue until Lasorda explained that he might be the only veteran on a five-hour bus ride to Miami for a Sunday exhibition.

"I'll do it tomorrow," Johnstone said.

To get primed for the annual test, Johnstone went to dinner with a couple of veterans. Rounds of beer followed, well past curfew.

The following day, Lasorda found Johnstone in the clubhouse and told him to report for his test.

The nurse behind the counter was an intimidating person. She had a cold, threatening personality and posed a challenge that a joker like

Johnstone could not pass up. As he walked into the training room, Johnstone grabbed an apple juice. In the bathroom, Johnstone filled the vial for his urine sample with the fruit juice.

With an audience of several minor leaguers waiting for their exams, Johnstone strolled toward the nurse. She saw the vial and remarked, "Mr. Johnstone. That sample looks rather dark."

Johnstone agreed.

"Madam, you're right," he said. "I better recycle it."

In the same style of downing a shot of wild turkey, Johnstone gulped the contents of the vial.

The nurse turned whiter than her uniform. Six rookies promptly went into hysterics.

"Moral of the story," Johnstone says, "life isn't always what it appears to be. Dads should try to set realistic goals for their children to reach. Talk the game with your young Little Leaguers. Avoid being critical of their play on the field.

"For every misjudged fly ball, your son or daughter managed to get into position to try and make the play. Why not focus on the good jump the outfielder had on the ball. That builds confidence.

"Confidence is what the game is all about. If someone believes in you, that's all you need to hear. Tommy Lasorda was a master at that. I recall one day Billy Buckner came to the ballpark. He looked half-dead.

"As you know, Billy Buck played in pain throughout his career with his bad knees and all. But this day, he was begging Lasorda for a day off because he was sick. Lasorda replied that it would be important for Buckner to dress for the game.

"Be ready," Lasorda said. "I may need you in the seventh or eighth inning to swing a bat."

"Buckner figured that he could do that. In batting practice, Lasorda asked Buckner to take a few swings. He also ran the bases. After his last hit, Buckner ran down to first base and found his glove waiting for him.

"Take a few ground balls," Lasorda said, "and then retire to the clubhouse."

"Buckner took a few grounders and then came into the trainer's room. A few minutes later, the trainer called for Buckner to get dressed.

"Why? I'm not playing. Lasorda said he might use me to pinch-hit in the late innings."

"Well," the trainer said, "you're in the starting lineup."

Buckner quickly put on his uniform. He headed down the runway and found Lasorda in the dugout.

"Bill," Lasorda said. "You took fielding practice, batting practice and ran before the game. I have confidence in you that you can play and help us win today."

That day, Buckner had a couple of hits and drove in a run to spark a 3-1 win over Cincinnati.

"I thought you were sick," Lasorda said. "I bet you feel better right now."

Live Your Dream

Every minor leaguer dreams of playing in the big leagues. So do the broadcasters.

Don Wardlow has been announcing minor league baseball games for a number of years. He's also only blind man who has broadcast a major league game and a professional fight.

"The perfect example of a willingness to work and to believe in yourself," New Britain owner Joe Buzas says. "If you are willing to pay the price of hard work, you can do anything."

Wardlow always dreamed of broadcasting baseball games. During his youth in New Jersey, his hero was New York Mets broadcaster Lindsey Nelson.

"Dad," he told his father, "I have to meet Mr. Nelson."

With help from the Mets public relations department, it was arranged that Wardlow would be able to talk with Nelson at the ballpark.

As the years passed, Wardlow mastered Braille and practiced announcing baseball games.

In college, he finally got the chance to broadcast. Since graduation, Wardlow has been broadcasting minor league games. One of his longer stints was with the New Britain Rock Cats.

"All fathers have the special ability to unleash great powers to their children," Wardlow says. "My father believed I could achieve anything I wanted to do. He never stopped me from dreaming."

Find a Phone

It can take less than a minute to telephone a parent and offer words that a child is doing something right. A concrete statement like "I saw your child help another youngster who fell" or "Your son had a 100 on his math quiz" takes just a few seconds.

In the course of a school year, I've made over 1,000 calls to parents. The reaction is great. If I hold onto the line for a few extra seconds after making that encouraging call, I often hear a father commenting to his wife: "It's the school principal. Our son had the highest mark on the English test!"

Dads, you can do the same thing. A telephone call may cost 25 cents, but your encouraging words are priceless. Stress the positives in the work your child is doing.

The Mentor

They came from different eras, different regions of the country and from different cultural backgrounds. One was 80 years old. The other was 25. One could hardly walk. The other could run like a thoroughbred from his native Kentucky.

The elder man had finished a five-decade teaching career in Connecticut. His last student was a young man who was taking courses for a career in education. The topics often discussed were baseball, school and the world.

The older gentleman was my father. He made it possible for Erwin Bryant, the younger man, to attend college. Now an executive with the Boston Red Sox, Bryant knows how important it is to have a mentor.

The two met when the younger man was honing his baseball skills in the Red Sox chain and played with the Bristol Red Sox of the Eastern League. When Bryant decided to enroll in college, he lived in my dad's house, often assisting him to get dressed or making a trip to the library to check out a book my father wanted to read.

The passion for baseball never left Bryant. My father sensed that and his love for the game bridged the friendship. When my dad died in 1988, Bryant was one of the pallbearers who carried my dad to his burial site. Mentors at any age can enrich someone's life.

The Fast Lane

"Sudden" Sam McDowell was known for his blazing fastball when he pitched in the big leagues, striking out over 300 men twice in his career and leading the majors in strikeouts six times. He credits his father, who worked as a metallurgist for U.S. Steel, for his ability to solve problems.

These days, McDowell, who overcame an alcohol and drug addiction, is employed by the Texas Rangers and Toronto Blue Jays as a counselor. He works with young players, offering ways to work through troubling times without drugs.

"Excuses don't solve problems," McDowell says. "People solve problems."

McDowell advises people to look at all sides of a situation before passing judgment. "You have to understand what the problem is and if it is of concern to you," he says. "You have the right to solve the problem any way you wish. . . as long as it does not bother another person."

With proper guidance, people can solve problems. "You can do anything you want but remember, there is a price to pay," McDowell says. "The price is hard work.

"I think fathers can help their children so much by setting up choices," he says. "A child must learn to solve problems for himself. And as a parent, you can assist in solving by making the choices such that a child learns through repetition."

Sam's special advice to children is to have no secrets. He gave this advice to my fifth grade students recently when he talked to them at school. When children keep secrets from their mom and dad, they are asking for problems. He advised the children to seek advice from teachers and counselors when someone tells them to keep a secret.

Dusty Knows Best

When he struck out three times in a park league game, eight-year old Dusty Baker wanted to quit playing baseball.

"Dusty," his father said, "maybe you'll get three hits tomorrow."

When Baker tried to get an increase in his allowance for routine chores around the house, his father balked.

"Dusty," his father said, "one doesn't earn money for being responsible in the home. One learns how to be disciplined for life."

Baker, who manages the San Francisco Giants, credits his philosophy on life to his father.

"You have to learn how to deal with the system and when to draw the line," Baker says. "Every person has an outer dignity. That's where you need the job and must listen to the other person. But there's also inner dignity. No job or person can take this away from you. A father has to teach his son when to stand up and not be afraid of conflict. The best way is to keep open lines of communication."

Baker believes the best teachers in the world are the elderly. "They can teach so much. They are waiting to be asked," he says. "You can learn from their lives. They have invested time and energy into this world. They have so much to offer.

"I see this absent in sports today," Baker says. "A young player can learn so much from picking the mind of a player who reached the big leagues. There are resources available but so few take advantage of them."

Ring the Bell

All-Star shortstop Jay Bell credits his father for "a strong foundation" in respecting authority, people and religion.

"I guess I was in the first grade when I found out about unconditional love," Bell says. "My father said he would 'Step in front of a bullet' for me.

"Every youngster wants the appreciation of his father," Bell says. "And to understand that your dad would lay his life down, you can't ask for bigger reinforcement that someone cares a great deal about you."

Like Father, Like Son

Bill Veeck was a master promoter in baseball, once signing a midget to a professional contract and setting off fireworks at the ballpark following a home run.

Like his father, Mike Veeck is doing the same thing in baseball at the minor league level in the Northern League.

"My dad taught me to be happy, curious and to be interested in other people's lives," Mike says. "You have to be intellectually courageous. Dads need to be generous of that spirit. It might seem a bit old fashioned but give your children an endless supply of warmth and love. It works."

Don't Pass the Buck

Manager Buck Showalter, in gearing up for his first season with the expansion Arizona Diamondbacks, often recalls the words he heard from his father about how important the family is to a successful life.

"There is nothing more valuable that you can give to your children than your time," Showalter says. "It's not so important what you do with them but find a way to spend time with them.

"My dad always gave his time to his children and stressed the family unit every day. One of the best things a father can do for his kids is to love their mom. It teaches the youngsters how to get along. Be consistent and treat people fairly."

Details and Honesty

Rollie Sheldon grew up on a farm in rural Connecticut where "my sister was better at milking cows than I was. That's how I wound up playing sports.

"My father," he recalls, "figured I had a better chance throwing a baseball or basketball."

In 1961, Sheldon won 11 games for the pennant-winning New York Yankees. He says the biggest boost he received that season was from veteran pitcher Ralph Terry who "just took the time to help rookies like me. The day after a game, the two of us would be in the outfield shagging flyballs. Ralph would review how I pitched each batter. That helped so much."

Another source of inspiration was pitching coach Johnny Sain.

"My second father," Sheldon says. "Here's a guy who taught you to visualize what you were going to do before you threw the ball. He would have me throw the day before a game to reinforce what I had to do when I took the mound."

Sheldon now makes his home in Lees Summit, Missouri. He has applied the techniques from baseball such as "preparing for situations before they occur" as a key in disciplining his children.

"Observe the best players on their teams and use them as a model to improve your ability," Sheldon says. "You might not be able to throw a baseball as fast but the work ethics or mental focus can help you think about situations and how to solve problems.

"You can help your children so much by applying this to parenting and discipline," Sheldon says. "Dads must mentally prepare themselves for a situation before they occur and work at a solution."

On Perseverance

Walt "Moose" Dropo often heard his father say "work hard and practice the trade in which you want to earn your living."

In 1950, Dropo, who could put a charge into a baseball, won the American League Rookie of the Year Award. He became one of the league's most feared sluggers.

"Ted Williams was a guy I watched like a hawk," Dropo says. "He was a master at establishing a foundation for self-discipline and setting goals. I did my best to copy Teddy Ballgame."

Dropo reminds dads to pattern the same skills a hitter develops in raising a family. "You need a foundation and must set goals," Dropo says. "If a youngster can visualize what must be done and practice every day, there will be success. You must be there because a father is the biggest influence for a child. Don't dwell on mistakes. Emphasis hard work and practice. Be a model for your child."

Take Out the Trash

Steve Lyons was a close friend of my family on his way to the major leagues. I recall a story he told me about his father who set a basis for doing chores around the house.

ALL-STAR DADS

"I was 12 years old," Lyons says. "I was watching a baseball game on television with my dad. He quietly asked me to bring out the garbage. I declined.

"My dad asked me to leave the TV room. I went to an adjacent room. My dad then asked me why I told him 'No.' I went into a long story about why was I picked to be the one to take out the garbage instead of one of my brothers. All I remember is my father saying 'You are going to bring out the trash. Don't make a fuss. Just bring out the trash.'

"I learned from that. There are basic rules a child has to master. It starts with being quiet and doing chores that a parent asks you to do. These non-negotiables must be in place for a child to feel secure."

Children need structure in their lives. It is up to the parent to establish the foundation of responsibilities and values.

Chapter 4
Huggin' Third

Calling 911

The school nurse talked to the kindergarten class and the focus of the discussion was a number to call for emergencies.

"You can save someone's life by dialing 9-1-1," the nurse aid. "It works. It helps people."

Though the nurse stressed that 9-1-1 should be used strictly for cases involving serious injuries, one youngster went home and told his younger brother what he learned in school that day.

"If something should happen," Teddy told his brother, "just dial 9-1-1. It's an emergency number."

Two days later, a policeman arrived at the family residence.

The officer in blue inquired if anyone at the house had dialed 9-1-1.

"Sir, not to my knowledge," the father said.

"Are there any youngsters here?" the policeman asked.

"Yes," the father said. "My young son is."

The officer wanted to talk with the child.

"Teddy," the policeman asked, "did you use the telephone?"

The boy nodded.

"Do you remember the number you dialed?" the policeman asked.

"I dialed 9-1-1," the boy responded. "My brother told me he learned in school that in cases of emergency, all you have to do is call that number."

"Teddy," the policeman said, "that number is for real emergencies, like if someone stops breathing."

"I had a real emergency," the boy said. "I asked my dad to help find my truck but he was real busy. That's why I called 9-1-1."

A child's panorama of the world differs from that of an adult. The differences stress the value of constant communication between a parent and a child. It's important for dads to channel energy at looking at the universe through the eyes of their children. It assists in the process and eases the burden for parents in setting workable examples for a child to make responsible decisions.

Penmanship Counts

A second grader was causing turmoil at home and at school with his handwriting. Bobby refused to slow down. He resisted using the little finger grip that was suggested to improve his form. The teacher's pointers did little to alter Bobby's penmanship.

The situation resulted in several heated and vocal discussions in class as well as at home involving assignments where neatness was part of the grade. To solve the problem, the parents began to work closely with the instructor. The result was a meeting at my office to determine the next step.

"Just tell the youngster the following," I said. "So sad. I know Mr. Reardon will not accept this type of work from you, so please go and see him. Maybe the two of you can work it out."

Following classes the next day, Bobby appeared at my office. He told me that his papers were a mess. He said he worked too fast and had difficulty with the pencil grip.

I told him not to worry. We would call his father to pick him up when his papers were done neatly.

"Bobby," I said, "I have all the confidence in the world in you."

I gave Bobby a big smile and set up a table where he could get to work.

Within an hour, Bobby slowly began to understand responsibility and what was required.

"Mr. Reardon. I'm getting hungry," Bobby said.

"So am I," I told the student.

Within an hour, Bobby's writing dramatically improved. He soon became a model student and earned a number of gold stars for his penmanship. In a nutshell, the child solved the problem, the solution that works the best.

When we have a "vision" for a child which goes beyond the child's imagination, we give him a challenge by giving him a definite goal. When Bobby knew the goal, he accepted the responsibility and had success.

Don't Forget To Call

Del Unser followed his father to the big leagues. He recalled seeing his dad do a number of odd jobs during the off season to support his family. Until the day he died of a heart attack at age 82, Del's father was still doing chores around the family dairy farm.

"My dad once told me, 'When you put on a baseball uniform, you will hustle all the time or it will come right off you,' " Del says. "I learned that lesson at a young age."

As an executive in baseball administration these days with the Phillies, Unser has reminded players in the Philadelphia chain about the importance of running out every ground ball or hustling out of the dugout to a fielding position. In addition, he suggests each player call home and talk with loved ones.

"My father was away from home yet he never missed a day calling to talk to my mom or his children," Del says. "That's something I did throughout my career. It works."

Take Time To Listen

Former big leaguer Tito Landrum has launched what he hopes becomes a second career as physical therapist. He often draws upon his baseball playing days, speaking to people about patience and dedication.

"Being able to talk is important but I believe the most important part of the communication process is listening," he says.

Landrum says what boosted his career was listening to coach Jimmy Piersall, a former outfielder who supplied the necessary confidence about playing the outfield.

"It was Jimmy," Tito says. "He talked about hard work and sacrifice. He preached communicating with other players so you know just how much ground to cover so no one gets hurt. I can't thank him enough."

Tito believes in perseverance. He understands the concept that what the mind believes becomes the truth and one can achieve goals. Under Piersall's encouragement, this was possible.

Fair, Not Equal

When my daughter Julie was seven years old, she saw her mother battling Crohn's disease, an intestinal illness that has no known cure or cause. Julie became interested in helping her mom and has pursued a career in medicine. She studied at Harvard, practiced medicine in Bangladesh and India and is now a doctor in Minnesota.

I mention this because Dr. Foggaballa, another physician, thinks he has mastered how to understand individuals.
One day, Dr. Foggaballa had three different patients. One had suffered a broken leg. Another was troubled by a toothache. The third had a sore toe.

Within 24 hours, Dr. Foggaballa scheduled operations at city hospital for each patient. All were to have their appendix removed.

Not surprisingly, each patient sought a different doctor.

"Why would you do that?" Dr. Foggaballa asked. "Is something wrong? I treat everyone equally."

It's wise to teach children at an early age about equality but it's more important to treat children fairly. Youngsters are different and must be addressed as individuals. Try to remember Dr. Foggaballa. I did in raising my three children.

Individualism Counts

Scott Bankhead pitched in the big leagues, making stops with both the Yankees and the Red Sox. He stresses the importance for a father to get to know his children as individuals.

"Be attentive to their dreams and their fears," he says. "Teach them responsibility and accountability for all their actions and decisions. Teach them to never quit and how to look for solutions to their own individual problems."

By being aware of your child you can help him spread his wings and
fly. Until he stretches himself toward a goal, he will never know how
far his abilities can take him.

Fleeting Time

Mike Andrews played for the Red Sox and White Sox during his
career. The former second baseman often talks about making time for
your children.

"Spend as much quality time as you possibly can with your
youngsters," he says. "They are going to grow up so quickly. You
cannot get those years back."

It seems that my children have grown so fast. The days when they
were little can never be recaptured, they are now three great adult
friends to me. Yesterday is often a blurred vision and tomorrow is an
unknown dream. Doesn't it make sense to enjoy today?

Flashbacks

There are times as Jimmy Watkins goes through parenthood that he
can hear his father's voice.

"My dad believed in discipline and working hard at being a dad,"
Watkins says. "He also did so much for building my confidence."

Self-esteem is critical for success and Watkins, who played in the
minor leagues and also managed in the Cape Cod Summer League, has
applied his father's philosophy in dealing with athletes as well as his
own children.

"I thank my father for putting a glove on my hand and having a
catch with me," he says. "My dad talked about the importance of hard
work and how it will lead to being successful. He had the courage to
remind me about working harder in ways where he used praise as a
tool to give guidance. There's a commitment to practice and hard
work."

Watkins has stressed to his children the difference between wants
and needs. Many items that are advertised on television are "wants"
and Watkins believes that parents must help their children understand
choices because "it teaches responsibility.

"What we do for one child doesn't necessarily mean we have to do the same for the other," Watkins says. "Just be fair and realize each child is very special."

Because each child is an individual, they give back to the world in an individual way.

Second the Advice

Hall of Famer Bobby Doerr says he acquired his philosophy of life from his father during his youth growing up in Oregon.

"Dads have to be honest and be of good character," Doerr says. "They have to work hard at whatever they choose to do and the dedication to hard work will lead to success in their lives.

"Stay true to your principles and your children will, too."

Every person can find happiness in the way they live their lives. We have to work on our attitudes and actions on a daily basis. Each individual has the solutions to his problems inside himself. If all dads followed Doerr's advice, what a wonderful world we would have.

Out of the Cold

The San Diego Padres were in the heat of a pennant chase and pitcher Bob Tewksbury knew every game mattered more than the previous one. What mattered more to his five-year old son, however, dwarfed the importance of throwing strikes to win a ballgame.

In the months leading up to the season, "Tewks" was in the role of "Mr. Mom" for his two children. His only break occurred when his wife would take the youngsters for a couple of hours. That enabled Tewksbury to run a few miles to build his stamina and leg power for spring training. He stressed how much he needed the free time, not only to exercise, but for mental relaxation.

It was after a jog one Saturday that Tewksbury's son was learning how to ice skate. In recent weeks, a chair had been used to assist the child. It is a way to help a novice maintain balance while learning how to glide on ice.

This particular lesson did not go well. The boy tried his best but he kept falling. He was a picture of discouragement.

From the stands, the boy's father, exhausted from running six miles and tending to his three-year old daughter, sensed the ride home would be tense. He kept hearing the voices of past ancestors, telling him if he wanted to quit, "be a quitter" and "You will disappoint not only yourself but the entire family." There would be tears and plenty of yelling.

The ice-skating session reached a conclusion. Tewksbury did his best to remain calm. His son was nearly in tears because of frustration.

It was only a few months ago that Tewksbury was struggling in the big leagues. He was unable to throw strikes consistently. Some kind words about hard work from a teammate supplied a boost of confidence. It helped Tewksbury get back in the proverbial groove.

"Griffin," he said to his son, "who scored six goals in a youth soccer game last summer?"

The boy's eyes sparkled.

"I did."

"And son, who is the best pitcher in the big leagues?"

"That's easy dad," the boy said. "You are."

"Who can get a hit off me any time?"

"I can."

The father and son hugged. Tears of joy replaced beads of sadness.

"Son,. I know you can skate. Let's try again."

The youngster, now somewhat relaxed, went back out to the rink. Over the next few minutes, young Griffin must have fallen a dozen times. With each slip, the boy cracked a smile as his father said, "Kerplunk."

Moments later, the only sounds were blades cutting the ice. The boy was staying on his skates. He found his stride and kept his balance.

"Dad," the boy cried. "I can skate. This is great. I can skate."

His father smiled to himself, "I finally know how to be a dad . . . and it's great."

Tewksbury had learned to turn a trying situation into one of great joy.

Saints and Sinners

Ron LeFlore epitomizes that mistakes are wonderful opportunities to learn. In his youth, he made a number of poor choices and spent time in prison for armed robbery.

During his confinement at Jackson State Prison, the Detroit Tigers scouted LeFlore who had the tools such as speed and good hands to play baseball. Upon Billy Martin's urging, the Tigers signed LeFlore in 1973 and he was soon a standout in the big leagues. The story of his life was eventually made into a movie entitled One in a Million.

The dramatic change made LeFlore's father a proud man. The elder LeFlore had worked hard to support his family as an artist. His son eventually followed his dad's creativity. Ron's stroke with a wand sent baseballs into orbit.

Ron LeFlore's determination made it possible to battle long odds. He reached the major leagues and became a success in a situation where many others might have quit. LeFlore, however, kept moving forward.

Like LeFlore, a friend of mine, Jim Mulligan also overcame great odds. Mulligan was a POW during the Vietnam Conflict. He spent seven years in solitary confinement. He was tormented physically and emotionally. Through it all, he developed a simple philosophy of life.

"There are only two types of people on this earth," Mulligan says. "Saints and sinners. The saints get up and try again."

It's important for dads not to get discouraged when a youngster bungles a school assignment or forgets to cover third base in a Little League game. Mistakes are part of growth. Miscues are fantastic opportunities for parents and children to learn about themselves and each other.

That's the view of Sal Yvars, a reserve catcher who played in the National League from 1947 to 1955. Yvars believes that if he made it through the maze of parenthood, any dad can be successful.

"If I could make it, anyone can," Yvars says. "I worked for 10 cents an hour as a boy in a nursery. I knew what it meant to work hard and put in long hours just to make a dollar. I didn't make money like the players make today in the big leagues during my era but I managed to put four children through college. I credit that to my upbringing and working within a budget."

Yvars summed up his parenting view with a reference to his youth in the nursery. "If you treat a tree right," he said, "it will grow straight and strong. If you don't, it will die off."

If dad puts forth the effort to help a child grow, a model is in place for a youngster to lead a good life.

The Right Words

Gorman Heimueller, a lefty who had a cup of coffee with the Oakland Athletics in the early 1980s, isn't afraid to admit that his dad is his best friend.

"I'm proud of that man," he says. "He's a special dad."

What Heimueller remembers most about his father is his dad's attention to detail and ability to supply words of encouragement.

"The man was always there to give me time and guidance," says the current pitching coach of the New Britain Rock Cats.

In working with pitchers in the Minnesota chain, Heimueller draws upon the advice he absorbed from his father.

"My dad knew the right things to say to me when I was upset," he says. "I learned so much from my father about dealing with people. He was able to guide as well as lead."

Taking Charge

Mike Heath, a former catcher, believes in taking responsibility for your actions, on the baseball field as well as in raising children.

"In baseball," he says, "if you're on first base and the batter hits a line drive that is caught by the first baseman, you cannot run to second base or you will be out. There is no discussion about that. You must correct it immediately so it doesn't happen again.

"You need to accept responsibility for your actions and like many young players and children, they must be taught with constructive criticism," Heath says. "Baseball teaches you three strikes and you're out. Family rules are non-negotiable. Teach children there is one strike and you're out. It's so important for a child to be responsible for any action. By doing this, you remove any excuse. There will be no manipulating others for your mistakes."

Heath recalls how teammate Dwayne Murphy patrolled center field for the Athletics. The Oakland Coliseum is one of baseball's toughest ballparks for outfielders because of its relationship to the sun. Several visiting players, as well as members of the home club, have difficulty in judging flyballs.

"I played a few games in the outfield and I credit Dwayne for helping me catch a ball," Heath says. "He practiced at becoming one of the best in the game. He gave me pointers and encouraged me to work at becoming better. I use that same philosophy with my children."

Believe in Role Models

Sid Hudson pitched a dozen years in the big leagues, starting with the Washington Senators in 1940 and winding up with the Boston Red Sox in 1954. He believes in solid values.

"God first, family second, and others third," he says.

Hudson also believes in role models.

"With the Senators," Hudson says, "my role model was Mickey Vernon. He was a real gentleman to other players and the fans."

It was during Hudson's career that he came in contact with legends of the game, people like Connie Mack, Bucky Harris and Clark Griffin.

During one of Hudson's final seasons, the team was playing the Philadelphia Athletics. He called for the hotel elevator to descend toward the locker rooms. The elevator went down a floor and stopped.

When the opened, Mr. Mack entered and said, "Good morning."

The ride continued and there was another stop.

The door opened and Elmer Valo, an outfielder for the A's, got on board.

"Good morning young man," Mr. Mack said. "Don't I know you?"

Valo replied, "Yes, Mr. Mack. I'm Elmer Valo, your right fielder."

The elevator door closed and the ride continued until it stopped on the next level.

Billy Hitchcock, an infielder with the A's, entered. Mr. Mack did not recognize who it was and asked "Don't I know you?"

"Mr. Mack," Hitchcock said. "I'm Billy Hitchcock. I'm your third baseman."

That day, Hitchcock batted in the third slot for the only time in his major league career. Though he did not get on base safely, Hitchcock, who batted .243 over his nine-year career, notes with a gleam that he brought an end to Mr. Mack's 50-year tenure as a skipper in the big leagues.

The respect and reverence that ballplayers held for Connie Mack never waned. Mr. Mack could teach and counsel his players with the schooling of seeing people and a game grow from the turn of a century. He was a father image for many players. He built champions and taught many how to be successful.

A Second Father

Jimmy Wynn's father taught his son the difference between right and wrong. The major point was listening to the teachers in school and doing homework assignments. School work had to be finished before playing baseball.

Wynn knows the importance of the family unit and how it must work to support each other.

"A simple 'I love you' means so much to a child," Wynn says. "I wonder what the future is going be for youngsters who don't hear that every day from their parents."

During his career, Wynn often talked with Walter Alston who managed the Los Angeles Dodgers for many years.

"Sit down son, and tell me how you feel," Wynn says. "That was Walter Alston. He was a second father to me."

Wynn, who played for the Houston Astros, was acquired by Los Angeles in a deal for pitcher Claude Osteen in 1973. When he arrived he had to change his uniform number.

Alston wore No. 1, the number Wynn had worn for many years with the Houston Astros.

"I had to change my number," Wynn says. "Walter told me 'Son, I know you have always worn the same number but I'm number one here so you can have the number which is one less than mine,' " Wynn says.

Keep Going Forward

Dave Beard pitched the pennant clincher in 1981 for the Oakland Athletics. He credits his father for all the success he achieved in baseball.

Beard's dad worked in the telephone industry for better than three decades. He found time to vacation with his family, often working overtime hours to afford it.

"My wife and I married very young and I made a commitment to her," he says. "We both had to learn lessons on how to listen and communicate. As a dad now, I am part of a team going through a learning process where I have to know when to direct and when to listen.

"I feel that sports have helped me because there are ups and downs in baseball much like there are ups and downs in family life. You learn from mistakes in the game. You learn about yourself and your family in dealing with mistakes in the home."

Just as children learn from their mistakes, so can adults.

Beard pitched seven years in the big leagues. He played for a number of managers.

"Billy Martin was my first manager and he managed by intimidation," Beard says. "You would tip-toe in the clubhouse. If you made a mistake, you were gone. He had success at first but his style was built for the short term. It divided the clubhouse.

"Steve Boros was a player's manager. He was a great communicator. He would come over and talk to you.

"Sparky Anderson was successful because he knew how to work with 25 different players. He was a true leader who knew how to treat each player fairly."

Beard says his dad did not pressure him into playing sports. With the lure of big money, some dads push their sons into athletics. They tend to spend more money than time to see youngsters excel.

"By the time many of these kids become teen-agers," Beard says, "they will be tired of sports. Instead of basketball camp, why not a family camping trip? My best childhood memories are going on vacation with my parents and sister."

Beard has worked hard at parenting. He often takes a ride with his children. They talk to one another in the car, working on the communication process of listening and discussing subjects.

"Take the time to be with your children," he says.

Rides in the Family Car

Steve Blass had his ups and down in the big leagues.

In 1971, he capped a great run by the Pittsburgh Pirates by winning Game 7 of the World Series.

Within three years, the right-hander, noted for exceptional control, could not find the strike zone with a compass.

"Life is full of surprises," Blass says. "It's how you react to a situation more than the situation itself."

Now in the Pittsburgh Pirates broadcast booth, Blass says his best time as a father is giving his children a ride back to college.

"It reminds me of the times I shared with my dad," Blass says.

Blass believes dads must slow down their lives and learn "how to relax," he says, "You need to be calm and in control of emotions to handle situations with your children."

Blass credits Danny Murtaugh for helping him and his teammates understand responsibility and working with others in a team concept.

"Danny often said it was up to us as players to do the things to win the ball game," Blass says. "Danny could manage with the best of them but he empowered his players to be important.

"Too often as parents we rescue our children instead of letting them solve their own problems," Blass says. "It's important to help your son or daughter but if you follow the old saying, 'Tell me and I'll forget. Show me and I'll remember. Let me do it and I will learn,' I believe you will empower your children with ways to be responsible and ways to deal with success and failure.

"I had a tendency to bail out my children and try to play the 'Super-Dad' role. They taught me quickly they wanted me as a consultant, not a lifeguard. They wanted to handle problems themselves.

"Dads must be the solid foundation for a child to grow. Give them confidence and stability and the knowledge that they will be loved, no matter what their success or failure is."

Remembering Mr. Yawkey

Ed Kenney grew up with the Red Sox and recalls discussions he overheard at Fenway Park between Mr. Tom Yawkey and his father, Ed Kenney Sr. "I was like a sponge," the current Bosox executive says.

Today as a father of two youngsters, Kenney often draws back on the words that Mr. Yawkey told his dad: "Treat players as individuals. Everyone is different so it's wise to learn to listen."

Much like his father, Kenney Jr. is involved in minor league development. Like his dad spent time offering advice to a player in the organization at the Class A or AA level, Kenney has followed his father's footsteps, not only in baseball but in the home.

"Listening is slowing down and being there for your son when he needs you," Kenney says.

Dads who master listening skills will help a youngster grow with patience, care and understanding for others.

Going the Distance

Bobby Taylor spent a portion of the 1970 season with the San Francisco Giants as a reserve outfielder. He says a man named James Irving was a major reason why he reached the big leagues.

"This man was my role model," Taylor says.

Taylor suggests that parents should be active in their communities as role models, as big brothers and big sisters.

"I often ask 'How many young men have you helped out during the last week?' " Taylor says. "We have to reach out and help others."

Taylor often talks about Dock Ellis, a former pitcher who has overcome his own demons and now helps others who are trying to get their lives back together.

"Dock has traveled miles to help a youngster," Taylor says. "He is trying to help one young man get his life in order. You don't have to travel across the country to help someone. There is likely someone in your neighborhood. Talk to that person. You can help."

Chapter 5
Over the Wall

Keeping in Contact

In baseball, there were a number of games when Dock Ellis threw a fastball and literally had little idea where it was going to go.

"I was a mess," Ellis says. "I was my own worst enemy."

Ellis went 138-119 over 11 seasons in the major leagues, most notably with the Pittsburgh Pirates and New York Yankees. In 1976, he was the American League's Comeback Player of the Year after winning 17 games in helping the Yankees to the American League pennant.

Since leaving baseball, Ellis has reformed his ways. He counsels youngsters about substance abuse. He works at building people's self-esteem. He stresses "being responsible because everybody makes mistakes."

Ellis made his share and he is thankful someone helped him.

"Someone took the time to help me mend my ways," he says. "My days are special because I'm working to help others. There is hope. You can be somebody. You can became a better person."

Ellis also has made the time to stay in contact with his children. It isn't easy considering the former big leaguer has been divorced three times, so he often uses the telephone.

"Stockholders of the phone company love me," Ellis says. "My monthly bill is a small fortune but to me, it's worth any price to talk to my children."

And talking is important for a child's growth. Ellis believes reading enables a youngster to explore the world and become equipped at lifetime skills of listening and speaking.

"I know being able to add and subtract are important but communication is the major building block," Ellis says.

Reading to his son, Ellis says, remains one of the biggest thrills he's had as a parent. Ellis would sit with his son and both would look at the pictures in the book. Each would then try to predict what would happen as the story unfolded.

"I think our stories topped the tale the author had created," Ellis says with a laugh. "In all seriousness, reading was a way for my son to learn about the world."

At a number of educational meetings, I have mentioned this concept to reading consultants. They praised the idea of parents always reading to their children. It is encouraged for all parents to read to their children because it amplifies one of the first steps in teaching a youngster to read.

Before a child can read from a book, he or she must follow the pictures and the rhythmic sound of the words. Add the fact that a youngster is taking part in a discussion, that combination has established a strong foundation in the education process.

Managing Time

The year Mickey Mantle broke into the big leagues in 1951, the American League Rookie of the Year was captured by one of Mantle's teammates.

Though Gil McDougald didn't have the great media buildup that accompanied Mantle's arrival to New York, he proved more than capable with the bat and glove. A five-time All-Star, McDougald won the AL's top freshman honor and went on to play for eight pennant winners during his 10 years with the Yankees. He could play either third, second or shortstop. He often delivered clutch hits. McDougald is the first rookie to ever hit a grand slam in the World Series.

"The little success I had in the big leagues," McDougald says, "I credit to the patience and work habits my father instilled in me."

In today's changing environment, McDougald believes it is very important for every father to address time management and take advantage of the hours with your children. "Teach them," he says, "to practice self-talk like 'I'm going to do my homework' or 'I'm going to help Dad rake the leaves.'

"You need to build confidence," McDougald says. "My dad always encouraged me to find a job that I would enjoy every day. Once you figure what you want to do, learn everything you can to advance your career in an organization. It involves hard work. The more you work, the more success comes your way. I believe that.

"I marvel at families today," McDougald says. "There are so many demands on working parents and that leaves little time for the most important things in your life like spending time with the people you love the most. But that's possible if you work at better time management.

"Mothers will always be the heart of the family. These days, too many moms are playing the father's role as well. I think it's important for children to know growing up that father is the head of the household. His authority must be respected. It is necessity that dad plays his part of being a leader each day at home."

Much like the afternoon in 1951 that McDougald tied a major league record with six RBI in one inning, he has a half-dozen suggestions for taking the helm of the household:

1. Plan morning and evening routines to reduces hassles
2. Limit time watching television and plan family fun activities
3. Set up systems so items such as keys or tools don't get lost
4. Plan activities with the children when you are not fatigued
5. Don't let phone calls dictate the family activities
6. Set dates when you can spend individual time with each child.

Jack of Diamonds

Jack Lamabe spent a half-dozen years in the big leagues as both a starter and a reliever. He had most of his success pitching in Fenway Park with the Red Sox, going 7-4 with a 3.15 ERA with six saves for Boston in 1963.

Now a minor league pitching coach in the Colorado Rockies organization, Lamabe believes silence is a learning tool for a dad because it is important to listen to your child. "His world is different than yours," Lamabe says.

"Care, credibility and love will motivate a young child," Lamabe says. "Every child is different and we must work with him using our own values."

While taking courses at Springfield College in Massachusetts, Lamabe spoke with Dr. Glen Olds, who was president of the liberal arts school and later served as a cabinet member during the Kennedy Administration.

Lamabe said that Dr. Olds felt that as an adult living in modern society, a parent should make the effort to use three game concepts when being with children.

"One game," Lamabe says, "involves competition where we play as hard as we can but we have the other person win. It favorably compares to the belief of Judeo-Christian society rather than the pagan philosophy of defeating an opponent at all costs.

"Another game is where parents work as hard as possible in a game against the children. It is based where parents compete as equals with children. There is no model for the child to follow. It is designed so the child leads.

"The last game is where the athletes compete and run the games themselves. Coaches work with the players during the week and will not be in the dugout on game day. Leadership would be in the hands of the captain."

Lamabe has two children and has a keen sense to understand the frailties of a young pitching prospect. "I listen more than I talk," he says.

In a way, Lamabe is a consultant, a role that he thinks would be make dads become better fathers.

"It requires the gift of time for your children," he says. "Reach out with all your skills and give your children time. Do that and children will learn to give time back to society."

The Three C's

Stan Williams often drew comparisons to Sandy Koufax and Don Drysdale in the Los Angeles Dodgers rotation. The big right-hander could throw as hard as Koufax. He also loved to pitch inside just like Drysdale.

During his early years in the majors, Williams was more a thrower than a pitcher. It was not until he finally understood the mental part of pitching, something he acquired by using Koufax and Drysdale as role models, that finally turned Williams around. Over the later portion of his 15-year career, Williams was one of the game's more dependable relievers.

"It took a while to realize you can maximize your talent through concentration, control and confidence," Williams says. "Increase one and the other two snowball."

Williams believes a "a person can improve performance" by setting goals and "apply yourself to do the best you can. Take a tip from watching successful people. It worked for me, not only on the baseball field but with my children."

Williams suggests parents should practice, visualize and discuss what they want to apply in family relationships much the same way a baseball player goes through the "repetition and adjustment process. "Call it a sorting out process to a degree," Williams says, "but it's more than that. It's a way to monitor your skills."

In working with children, Williams believes in total communication. "Do not assume anything," he says. "If you work with your children and tell them what you expect, there's a good chance what you want to happen will happen.

"If you assume a child can do a certain task.," Williams says, "and the youngster has no prior knowledge of how to do that chore, the result falls short at both ends. It could be something as simple as making a bed. The child becomes frustrated. You, as a parent, may say something that's emotionally charged. Why not show your son or daughter how it's done? Set up a situation where the choices are clear. Guide the child along.

"Learn to listen to your children. If you concentrate on teaching your child, and control yourself emotionally during the learning process, you have given your son or daughter the confidence to grow and handle all challenges."

Building Self-Confidence

As a youngster, Steve Hamilton loved baseball and dreamed of one day playing in the major leagues. "I spent hours throwing a ball against the house and helping the Yankees win another pennant," Hamilton recalls.

The dream came true for the tall left-hander who was an effective pitcher out of the bullpen for the Yankees, a specialist who had a nasty slider that often froze hitters, especially left-handed ones.

Today, Hamilton is the athletic director at Morehead State in Kentucky. He also coaches the university's baseball team.

"My greatest thrill," he says, "was being able to coach my sons at the collegiate level."

Hamilton played for a number of managers in the big leagues and meshed the concepts of Ralph Houk and Chuck Tanner.

"I played for a number of managers and my favorite one is Houk," Hamilton says. "Everyone called him the 'Major' because of his heroic deeds in World War II. Ralph knew how to keep the regulars and the reserves feeling as if they were part of the team effort. He made his players feel special. All of us need a confidence boost.

"Tanner had a way with getting the most from his players by leaving them alone," Hamilton says. "He had 25 different sets of rules for 25 different players. Athletes are self-starters. Tanner's style worked as a motivational tool because competitive people perform best when they are treated not only fairly but as individuals.''

As a youngster, Hamilton says his parents, who later divorced, never discouraged him from playing sports. Baseball became an avenue of expression and of motivation. "My parents were always supportive but when they separated, it did give me a feeling of inadequacy," Hamilton says. "I become more competitive as a player. I was more driven, almost to the point that I believed it was the only way I could be accepted as a person.

"Society has changed plenty over the last 25 years," Hamilton says. "What hasn't changed is that children need their best coaches at a young age. Have patience. Be understanding. Encourage your children."

Practice, Practice, Practice

Mike Heath, who manages in the Chicago White Sox chain, has discussed with me the basic lack of baseball knowledge that today's younger players possess. When I discussed this concept with Sam

McDowell, he stated that big league players of the 1950's and 1960's had played over 5,000 hours of baseball before they reached the majors, roughly 10 times the hours that have become the measuring stick for today's generation.

I have asked friends to telephone me whenever they see baseball being played without adult supervision. My phone seldom rings. Youngsters, it seem, do not take the initiative to play baseball to improve skills or as a simple interaction with other children.

The point here is being equipped for any situation. The more dad and mom can discusses workable options for their children, the easier it will be to handle any emergency or crisis. In sports, much like parenting, the answer is **PRACTICE, PRACTICE, PRACTICE.** Athletes often visualize how well they will perform before taking the field. They also practice to fine-tune skills. Doesn't it make sense for a father to do the same?

Say It Only Once

When parents use words as guidelines, it only helps a child grow. You establish a framework for a youngster who may test the limits at times but may opt to stay within the rules if addressed properly after the first offense.

Tony Lupien played first base in the big leagues for three different clubs in the 1940's and later coached baseball at Dartmouth College. He has seen a litany of players and managers handle adversity through athletics. He believes by setting limits, especially in one-on-one situations, you establish a point on the compass toward career success.

"If you have to remind a person over and over to do a chore," Lupien says, "you should be wise enough to realize that you didn't do it right the first time."

During his playing days, Lupien recalls that his parents never criticized a coach. "There would be discussions," he says, "but the drift I received at a young age was to be supportive of the school and of the teachers."

Lupien says he learned a major lesson in basketball. As a freshman, Lupien contributed to the team's success and wanted a memento of the year. When the scholastic season was over, he decided to keep his uniform.

Lupien's mentor at the time was Hugh Greer who later went on to coach at the University of Connecticut. During the annual sports assembly where the athletes are recognized and received letters, Lupien was smiling. He was waiting for the moment coach Greer called his name. Seated with his parents, Lupien sat in a state of shock as the ceremony drew to a close and Greer had not summoned him to the podium. Lupien's parents never said a word about the incident. Either did his coach.

The next day, a few minutes before school started, Lupien went to see his coach. He also had his basketball uniform neatly folded.

"That happened when I was 14 years old," Lupien says. "That was greatest lesson I learned about responsibility."

Do It Right

Spec Shea broke into the big leagues with a splash in 1947. As a rookie, he won 14 games for the New York Yankees, started the midseason All-Star Game. He later notched two victories in the World Series in helping the Yankees turn back the Brooklyn Dodgers.

"It was the type of year," Shea recalls, "no matter what I did turned out right. It was a type of season I wish every player could have."

Shea spent eight years in the big leagues. He feels the biggest parenting lesson he learned came from his days in the minors pitching for Eddie Sawyer.

"People remember Eddie for the Whiz Kids in Philadelphia in 1950," Shea says, "but that man set me straight."

A couple of days after a starting assignment, Shea would be summoned into Sawyer's office.

"When you expected it," Shea said. "Eddie would call you in and point to areas where you needed to improve. Eddie would not manage, discipline, or teach a player if "Lilly" was loose. He knew that when people are upset is not the time to teach. He would see a flaw in a recent game and stress how important it was to plan ahead. He wanted you to think before you went into action. I can still see him sitting in the dugout and point to his head. He was reminding me to think.

"It may sound off the wall but Eddie was able to build confidence in his players. He found a way to get you to believe in yourself," Shea says. "If you don't believe in yourself, nobody else can. As a dad, that's the most important point to consider in working with children. Encourage a child. Build on the strong points. You can give a child freedom to a degree but give them your time. That's the greatest gift you can give.''

One Country at a Time

Dave Gavitt left his imprint on college athletics by creating a basketball conference known as the Big East in 1979 that quickly established itself as one of the marketing successes in sports. It was Gavitt's foresight to put an entertainment package together that maximized exposure during the growth of regional sports cable networks. The made-for-television league not only generated revenues in the millions of dollars but became a recruiting tool other college conferences envied.

"We had a plan and found others who believed it could work," Gavitt says.

Vision, coupled with hard work, is a formula often associated with successful people. It is also a way for dads to teach their children to achieve goals.

"Character is caught," Gavitt says. "It can't be taught or bought. You must have a concern for others. That's why it's so important to have role models."

It was during his collegiate days that Gavitt recalls a coach named Julian telling a story about a youngster asking his father to have a catch with a baseball in the backyard. The boy was asked to wait but the child kept asking his dad to put the newspaper down and play. The father asked his son if he would put together a jigsaw puzzle before they went outside. The child agreed.

In a flash, the father found a geography teaser. He put the maze of pieces on the kitchen table. If solved properly, the result would be a map of the world. "That should keep you busy," he said, leaving the youngster and heading back to the television room.

As dad got comfortable in his rooting chair and anxiously awaited the opening pitch of a showdown game between the Red Sox and Yankees, the youngster soon appeared with his glove.

"Finished already?" the father asked.

His son nodded.

"I must have a genius," he said to the boy.

The boy smiled.

"How did you figure out where Asia and South America are?" quizzed the father.

"Dad, it was easy," the boy said. "I made the reverse side of the puzzle," he said.

"You what?"

"Dad, it was a picture of a little boy looking out his window toward the heavens," the youngster said. "Once I assembled the boy, the rest of the world was a snap."

Making a Choice

Milt Bolling had the ability to play shortstop on a regular basis but a series of elbow and leg injuries reduced his career to that of infield utilityman. He played for the Boston Red Sox and Detroit Tigers during a seven-year hitch in the 1950's.

"There is no ballpark like Fenway Park," Bolling says.

There may have been no other player who could hit with power like Ted Williams.

"When people think of the Red Sox," Bolling says, "they think of Ted Williams."

One afternoon in the tight ballgame, Bolling was at-bat with a chance to win the game. With the faithful roaring on a 2-2 pitch, Bolling geared up for a fastball but was overmatched. He swung through for the third strike.

As he headed back to the dugout, all he could see was Teddy Ballgame glaring at him. Bolling soon got an earful from Williams, a run-on sentence of colorful verbs and selected portions of the human anatomy.

Williams wanted to know why Bolling had neglected to hit the pitch for the game-winning hit.

"Ted, I knew what was coming but I did not have the ability to hit that pitch," I told him. "I'm sorry."

Williams could not understand Bolling's frustration of failure. He says he has seen the same from many dads who struggle to comprehend the problems a child faces in growing up.

In his youth, Bolling recalls the strong bond that he and Frank, his brother who also played in the big leagues with Detroit and Milwaukee, had with their father.

Milt wanted to play football but his father sought to set some limits for the boys because of the injury factor. The decision hinges on "either play football or you can play baseball and basketball," Milt says. "The answer was easy. I picked two sports over one."

Bolling believes a father can overwhelm a child with unrealistic guidelines and "it makes no sense to set up a youngster for failure," he says. "Give your son or daughter the gift of time. Work with your children. Be a role model. Do things together. Listen to them. Be supportive."

Open Door Policy

Al Newman played in the big leagues with the Montreal Expos and Minnesota Twins. These days, the former utilityman is coaxing the New Britain Rock Cats of the Eastern League to hone their skills to climb the baseball ladder.

"My door is always open," Newman says. "It's a good policy because young players often struggle."

Newman has tried to set limits for his players. They often work but when a player is in a slump, "a manager must know his players to handle situations and each individual personality. I can suggest something to a player once or twice, and he will usually understand. With another player, it might take a few more times. There is a fine line there about being non-negotiable. At the same time, you must have respect for other people."

As a parent, Newman suggests that dads must understand themselves first and then will be equipped with relating to others. "Your children are individuals," Newman says. "Set an example for them as much as you set rules. Don't withdraw if they fail. Work with them."

Woodling's Advice

Gene Woodling won four batting titles in the minor leagues and was a valuable platoon player for the New York Yankees. He was also among a handful of Yankees to play on five consecutive World Series champions (1949 to 1953).

"Casey Stengel had a way with creating an image that was good for baseball," Woodling says. "He was a tremendous public relations man but once the game began, he was tough. Do it right or you were gone. He was the boss. No excuses."

Woodling wishes fathers of all ages would teach responsibility and discipline to their children.

"It's a lost art these days," Woodling says. "If my dad asked me to do something, he just said it once."

In the classroom, it was the same.

"If I complained about it," Woodling says, "I knew my punishment would be more severe at home than at the principal's office.

"I still believe children want to learn what's right and what's wrong but dads don't seem to have the time to teach it to their children. And when someone tries to do it, there's a lawyer or a member of the media making it impossible. This is not the America I grew up in."

Woodling knows it's difficult for parents but discipline must start in the home. Woodling says. "A good start is to look in the mirror."

"When I played in the big leagues, I was away 80 days from my children," he recalls. "But the time I was home, I was there to help them, to teach them respect and to be good citizens. I can't believe we don't pledge the flag or have prayers in our schools today.

"Look at baseball. When I was kid, athletes respected fans and would never do things to misguide a youngster. I played for the Yankees and there was pride to put that uniform on. We were concerned about image and what was going on in the country. Athletes used to take their responsibility seriously to be role models for young fans."

"I know I'm sounding like I'm from a different age but people today have less pride in themselves and in what they do. If you don't believe you are something, what message are you sending to your son or daughter. Dads, it's up to you to get back to basics. Be a leader. Take charge. You can be somebody. You can be the role model your child needs.''

Chapter 6
Post-Game Pointers

Have You Seen This Guy?

This dad worked very hard to make sure his son had success in sports. He pushed the child from an early age and throughout his teen years. The youngster's resentment to his dad is overwhelming. The philosophy expressed in the following list has led to lifetime of emotional problems for other members of the family:

1. Force your son to play sports
2. Take your aggression out on your son
3. Live through your son's successes
4. Be your son's severest critic
5. Play the watchdog over your son
6. Lecture your son about his games
7. Always push him to have more success
8. Always find a mistake in whatever he does
9. Demand perfection
10. Be overbearing

The following concepts are ones which I have drawn from conversations with ballplayers, coaches and others. It is my hope that these pointers will serve as a guide for all dads to become better and patient fathers.

ALL-STAR DADS

Al Newman, current manager of the New Britain Rock Cats

1. Have Mom and Dad talk together when they talk to the children.
2. Realize anger is a way to manipulate a person's behavior.
3. Practice what you say before you discipline.
4. Children need structure.
5. Realize when you are tired is when you lose your temper.
6. Put in time with your children.
7. Set up "dates" for special time with your children.
8. Read to your children.
9. Realize children learn best by doing.
10. What you model is what your children will follow.

Greg Gross, former outfielder who ranks among the game's top pinch-hitters

1. Don't put children on pedestals for sports.
2. Don't find excuses for children.
3. Teach children to do their best and accept the results.
4. Teach you can learn more from defeat than from wins.
5. Model how important you and your wife are for the family.
6. Parenting is hard work but be available for the children.
7. Read to your children.
8. Teach your child how to think.
9. Teach your children to have pride in their work
10. Control your temper.

Nelson Briles, former pitcher and community liason for the Pittsburgh Pirates

1. Your word is always your bond.
2. Time is the gift to give, not money.
3. Give children jobs around the house.
4. Have meals together.
5. Honest day's work for honest day's pay.
6. Family needs structure and discipline.
7. Men should serve as mentors to other men.
8. Religion gives structure to the family unit
9. Don't be afraid to hug your child.
10. Talk with your children.

Earl Weaver, Hall of Fame manager

1. Do not underestimate the importance of religion
2. It's what you learn **AFTER** you know it all that counts

Dick Radatz, former bullpen ace of the Boston Red Sox

1. Always give 100 percent
2. Honesty.
3. At times of crisis, think before you act.
4. Take time to know your child.
5. Practice for sports and practice for life problems.
6. Let children play baseball without adult interference.
7. Be fair.
8. Give children your attention.
9. Don't expect your children to be something they are not.
10. Give love and attention.

Mike Heath, current manager of the Winston-Salem Warthogs

1. Dads should give leadership to their families.
2. Religion has to be an important part of the family.
3. Have fun limits.
4. Teach responsibility.
5. No excuses.
6. Don't blame others for your mistakes.
7. Mom and Dad should be in communication together with their children.
8. Focus on doing a good job on everything.
9. Honesty.
10. Always do your best.

Ron Diorio, former pitcher for the Philadelphia Phillies

1. Dads should give encouragement and time to their children.
2. The family is the focus point of life.
3. Dads should be fun.
4. Family meals are important.
5. Families should have a great deal of love.
6. Dads should give love to their children.
7. Dads have to be reliable and be the strength of the family.
8. Grandparents are very important.
9. Dads give security to the family.
10. Thank God for your blessings.

Dock Ellis, former pitcher now involved in substance abuse counseling
1. Dads be willing to help your neighbors.
2. Love your children.
3. Advice for Divorced Fathers:
    a. Stay in contact daily by phone with your children.
    b. Write them letters.
    c. Have overnight stays for your children.
    d. Keep open the lines of communication.
    e. Give time to your children.
    f. Serve as a "role model" for your children.
4. Teach that school is important.
5. Learn to listen to your children.
6. Teach the children the word, "NO."
7. Read to your children.
8. Take parenting classes. This takes courage.
9. Use other Dads as mentors. Ask for help.
10. It's O.K. not to know, but it's not O.K. not to ask for help.

Dr. Julie Reardon, Riverside Hospital of Minneapolis, Minnesota
1. God did not give us the 10 suggestions. He gave us the 10 Commandments.
2. Have family meals together.
3. Have chores for family members.

Gene Woodling, member of New York Yankees champions (1949-1953)
1. Children need discipline and guidelines.
2. Give time to your child.
3. Teach your child responsibility.
4. Support your children's teachers and school.
5. Dads and men have to be the leaders and take responsibility for their children.
6. The home is where discipline is learned.
7. Know you are a role model for your child.
8. Teach your children to respect others and other's belongings.
9. Know your neighbors and have neighborhood picnics.
10. Dads, take pride in yourself and job.

Vernon Law, 1960 NL Cy Young Award winner

1. Believe in respect and firmness.
2. Support your child.
3. Have jobs for children.
4. Teach "values" to your children when they are young.
5. Develop "Good Habits" and discipline when young.
6. Learn by example especially about drugs and alcohol.
7. Communication is important in a family.
8. Develop your child's strengths.
9. Teach your child responsibility.
10. Have firm guidelines.
11. Parents have to stick together, support each other and model your love for your mother.
12. Children need security from their Dad.
13. Dads, be involved in family instruction.
14. Discipline with Love. Let them know you dislike the behavior and love them.
15. Dad's love is unconditional.
16. We need to be open and learn from each other.

Billy Hitchcock, former manager of Detroit, Baltimore and Atlanta

1. Brother and sister take responsibility for the family.
2. Honesty, Integrity, and tell the truth.
3. Good Christian parents make good role models.
4. Always do the best you can.
5. Teach responsibility for chores.
6. Children need directions and guidance.
7. Talk to children gently, but firmly.
8. Know the right time to talk to children.
9. Know the right time to talk to the family.
10. Don't embarrass a child.
11. Grandfathers give love to grandchildren.
12. Grandfathers give time to listen to talk with your grandchildren.

Bob Gebhard, general manager of the Colorado Rockies

1. Work hard at whatever you choose to do in life
2. Be available to assist your children make choices, but allow them the freedom to choose a career path

Bill Gullickson, former big league pitcher

1. Establish goals for your family and stay focused on your goal.
2. Learn from mistakes and turn setbacks into wins.
3. Take care of yourself.
4. Plan family activity.
5. Children see what you do and will use you as a model.
6. Have a strong spiritual background.
7. Parents give time, not money.
8. Money should not be taught as a base of self worth.
9. The best time to answer a child's question is when he asks. Try to have both sides relaxed.
10. Talk with children about the best and funniest thing they did each day.
11. Tell children stories about grandparents and great grandparents.
12. Children are starving for discipline. Learn how to say "No."

Sandy Alderson, president and general manager of the Oakland Athletics

1. Hard work overcomes many shortcomings.
2. Spend less time worrying about deficiencies and more time overcoming them.
3. Know your deficiency and develop strength to overcome it.
4. Know what you can control.
5. Control your level of effort.
6. Dads, enjoy your children.
7. Be more available to your children than other dads.
8. Have time work with you.
9. Listen and communicate with your children.
10. Within structure, know how to be flexible when disciplining children.

Bob Tewksbury, pitcher for the Minnesota Twins

1. Routines are important in parenting.
2. Communication is important with your spouse.
3. Learn your children's traits and moods.
4. Share you duties with your spouse.
5. Take a deep breath at time of crisis.
6. Parenting is the best of all worlds.

7. Each child is completely different.
8. Parents need a break from the children.
9. Greatest job in the world is parenting.
10. Anything which is worthwhile does not come easily, and parenting is not easy.
11. Dads need role models and good friends.
12. Stay calm and peaceful with self talk.

Ned Garver, 20-game winner on the 1951 St. Louis Browns who went 52-102

1. No excuses.
2. Have reasonable rules.
3. Enforce rules.
4. Do the best job you can do.
5. Learn from your mistakes.
6. Set a good example by being a good role model.
7. Give every child jobs to do.
8. Teach a work ethic.
9. Communicate with your children.
10. Compliment your children (some children need more).
11. Every child is different.

Steve Hamilton, former pitcher and collegiate coach at Morehead State

1. Encourage your children to succeed.
2. Teach your child by "Self Motivation."
3. Support your child.
4. Don't push your child to be another you.
5. Learn to listen to your child.
6. Have patience and understanding.
7. Teach children to play games for fun.
8. Have understanding for your child when things go wrong.
9. Always do your best.
10. Have structure in your family.

Dick Balderson, vice-president-player personnel of the Colorado Rockies

1. Make sure you married a good woman.
2. Love your spouse.
3. Want to have children.

ALL-STAR DADS

4. Realize there will be bumps in the road.
5. Know you can get into a slower lane.
6. Good communication with all family members.
7. Create guidelines and rules.
8. Know what children can accomplish and let them understand what is expected.
9. Give children responsibility and make sure they understand goals.
10. Teach respect, honesty, and self-discipline... and model them for children.

Walt Dropo, 1950 AL Rookie of the Year

1. Have great respect for teachers and authority figures.
2. Parents should support teachers.
3. Love is more important than the dollar.
4. Model hard work and perseverance.
5. Set high goals and focus on them.
6. Children should have jobs.
7. Practice, practice, practice academic and sports skills.
8. Have realistic values and principles.
9. Have high standards for right and wrong.
10. Show love and caring before you discipline a child.
11. Tell your child you love them and model a good life.
12. Don't expect others to raise your child.

Tom Grieve, former Texas Rangers general manager and broadcaster

1. Teach your child responsibility.
2. Don't try to do everything for your child.
3. Don't try to make your child perfect.
4. Stand back and let your child learn from a mistake.
5. Give your children 100 percent support in what they want to do.
6. Love and support must be the motives in working with your child.
7. Have firm limits and boundaries.
8. Best lesson for dad: Be totally responsible for all you do in life and don't look for an excuse. Be totally accountable for what you do.
9. Listen to ideas from other parents.

Joe Morgan, manager of 1988 AL East champion Boston Red Sox

1. Respect authority at all levels
2. Find time for your children if it is a catch in the backyard or to help on a school assignment

John Reardon, Part I

1. Compliment the parent when you observe a well-behaved child.
2. Remember that misbehavior is often a child's way of saying "Show me that you love me."
3. Let your children overhear you saying nice things about them to other adults.
4. If you want children to turn out well, spend twice as much time with them and half as much money.
5. When no great harm will result, let your children do it their way even if you know they are wrong. We learn more from our mistakes than our successes.
6. Find something to praise in your child every day.
7. Don't brag about one of your children in the presence of another
8. Don't decide anything when you are angry.
9. Never watch a movie in front of your children involving activities you don't want them doing.
10. Don't overschedule your child's extracurricular activities.
11. Put up a basketball hoop in your yard.
12. Get your child a library card.
13. Work to improve your marriage.
14. Treasure your children for what they are, not what you want them to be.
15. Develop a secret family sign that says, "I love you."

John Reardon, Part II

1. Judge your success as a parent to the degree your children feel safe, wanted, and loved.
2. Children need a lot more smiles and hugs than lecture and instruction.
3. Convince your children that your love is not based on their performance.
4. Criticize the behavior, not the child.
5. When you make a mistake, admit it quickly and apologize.
6. Let your children help you work, even if it slows you down.
7. Spoil your spouse, not your children.
8. No secrets.

9. Remember your words can deeply hurt.
10. Leave notes in unexpected places that tell your children how much he or she is loved.
11. Mark on a door the birthday heights of your children.
12. When your children talk to you, put down the book or turn off the television.
13. Remember that the more a child feels valued, the better his values will be.
14. Have family meetings.
15. Take each child on a "special date" with Mom or Dad.

Stan Williams, former pitcher and big league pitching coach

1. Dads, work to improve each day, month, year.
2. Dads, study successful dads.
3. Dads, set goals.
4. If you have not told children what to do, do not expect them to do it.
5. Don't assume children know everything you know.
6. Prepare your children for problem situations.
7. Don't discipline your children when you are angry.
8. Know how to correct your mistakes.
9. Learn how to relax.
10. Learn the three C's
    A. Concentration - staying focused.
    B. Control - control yourself.
    C. Confidence - think about positive thoughts and feelings.

Steve Blass, former pitcher and current broadcaster

1. Keep life's lessons simple.
2. Teach what is right or wrong.
3. Don't forget where you came from.
4. Know how to talk and communicate, don't be afraid to talk with your children.
5. Talk in a comfort zone with your child until you feel comfortable to talk in other areas.
6. We don't have training as dads. We should call "time out" on life and enjoy our children.

7. Dads who make mistakes in parenting should not quit, but keep trying.
8. Teach self-motivation to your child.
9. Give your children as much time as you can. Time is something like throwing gum against the wall. The more you throw gum, the better chance you have of having it sticking. The more time you give a child, the better chance a child can learn.
10. You will be judged on how well you spent your time with your children.

Sam McDowell, consulting therapist for Major League Baseball

1. No secrets.
2. Learn to be a problem solver.
3. Think and understand other people.
4. Do not be judgmental.
5. No excuses.
6. You can do anything you want through hard work.
7. The child is like a sponge and the child's idol is the father.
8. Never talk down to a child.
9. Children should be respected.
10. Mistakes are where we can learn.

Gorman Heimueller, pitching coach of the New Britain Rock Cats

1. Be a good friend to your children.
2. Be there for your children.
3. Show affection to your children.
4. Be nice and fair to everyone.
5. Set limits.
6. Have the ability to listen.
7. Delay consequences.
8. Finish conversations on a positive note.
9. Learn from mistakes.

Al Oliver, 1982 NL batting champion

1. Spiritual guidance.
2. Strong discipline.
3. Responsibility.

4. Be well organized.
5. Be a good role model.
6. Have family get-togethers.
7. No excuses.
8. Love and security.

Dale Murphy, NL MVP in 1982 and 1983

1. Parenting is the hardest job in the world.
2. Parenting is the greatest adventure you can have.
3. Parenting is the greatest joy.
4. You need patience.
5. You need team work.
6. You need creativity.
7. You need commitment.
8. You need planning.
9. You teach responsibility.
10. Children need chores.
11. Work teaches self-esteem and problem solving.
12. Model and teach honesty and being a good person.
13. Parents make sports fun for the children.

Dusty Baker, manager of the San Francisco Giants

1. Respect grandparents and other older persons.
2. Unless a child respects you, he will not listen.
3. Assign children chores.
4. Go to church as a family.
5. Never quit.
6. Learn to deal with failure.
7. Love is discipline.
8. Have firm limits and consequences.
9. Stand up for truth and dignity.
10. Accept responsibility.
11. Respect your fellow man.

Art Howe, manager of the Oakland Athletics

1. Have respect for others
2. Be honest in all dealings with people
3. Stress the importance of moral values

Bud Selig, commissioner of baseball

1. Make the effort to spend time with your children
2. Develop a relationship with your children so they learn about life
3. Supply the necessary security for your family
4. Be patient
5. Believe in the values resulting from hard work

Jack Lamabe, roving pitching coach for the Oakland Athletics

1. Guide children within your family rules.
2. Model a good work ethic.
3. Teach the child school and education are very important.
4. Realize silence is golden and learn to listen.
5. Realize all your children are different.

Del Unser, director of player development for the Philadelphia Phillies

1. Have a tremendous wife.
2. Model hard work.
3. Realize the value of the individual child.
4. Call home and talk with your child every day if you are away.
5. Discuss your ideas.
6. Save energy to be a good dad.
7. Always do your best.
8. Realize the importance of time.

Dave Beard, former pitcher for Oakland, Seattle and Chicago Cubs

1. Be there for your child and discuss the day's events with him.
2. Give the child guidelines and steer him in the right direction.
3. Go for rides and talk with him.
4. Help him establish goals.
5. Parents, don't live your dreams through your child.
6. No pressure on children playing sports.
7. Learn to listen and communicate.
8. Create memories for your child.
9. Be dedicated to your marriage.
10. Sports teaches a child to cope with success and failure.

ALL-STAR DADS

Ralph Houk, manager of 1961-62 World Champion New York Yankees

1. A commitment to hard work
2. Spend time with your children
3. Read to your children so they learn about the many worlds around them

Dave Duncan, pitching coach of the St. Louis Cardinals

1. Be honest with your children
2. Have respect for other people and their property
3. Judge others on their relationship with you, **NOT** from what others might say
4. Appreciate the values involved in the family structure and the sacrifices made by your parents
5. Support your children with words that build confidence and love

Jake Gibbs, former catcher and baseball coach at Mississippi State

1. Do things as a whole family
2. Respect others
3. Spend time with your children
4. Offer examples of success
5. Hard work develops confidence and accomplishment

Epilogue

Dads can make a tremendous difference in the lives of their children. When a dad changes the way he communicates with a youngster, it will have a rippling, positive effect on the 21st century. Dads who control their tempers and keep a sense of humor will be on their way to raising happy children.

Some of the techniques featured in the text can be expanded from materials which can be obtained from the Love and Logic Institute based in Colorado. Consultant and educator Jim Fay has given each dad a place to start. It is hoped that this book helps all dads enjoy, love and give guidance to children everywhere. For more information contact:

The Cline Fay Institute
2207 Jackson Street
Golden, CO 80401
Phone: (800) 338-4065

ACKNOWLEDGMENTS

There are so many people to thank for making this book become a reality. It has been a team project and an exciting adventure.

To my wife Josie and our three children - Sue, Julie, and John - thanks for your great support.

To Erik Matthews and Mark Conway. Your generosity of time and enthusiasm made the journey possible.

To Jim Fay, many high fives to you because it was you who believed my ideas on parenting belonged between the covers of a book.

To Jack, Janice, Patrick and Nolan Lautier of Glacier Publishing, thanks for the chance.

To Sue Pettit, Bob Fox, and Reiko Uchida, special thanks for use of selected materials.

To all the players and coaches who contributed their comments, you are forever mentors. Continue to encourage others.

And finally, a tip of the cap to Mike Keating, Phil Lewis, Dusty Baker, Nelson Briles, Sam McDowell, Ron LeFlore and Dock Ellis. You are champions in every way.

ABOUT THE AUTHOR

A dynamic innovator of special parenting and motivational programs, **John Reardon** has hosted radio talk shows and a weekly television show on cable television called <u>Raising Children and Having Fun</u> in Connecticut. Currently the principal at Mountain View School in Bristol, Reardon has spent three decades in public education. He and his wife, Josie, raised three children through the methods contained in this book.

John Reardon

Author of **All Star Dads**
presents Parenting Lecturers and Workshops
> **"Being a Dad"**
> **"Having Fun and Raising Children"**
> **"Teaching Responsibility"**

> For information on availability
> the author can be reached by mail:
> 386 Ivy Drive
> Bristol, Connecticut 06010
> or by telephone (860) 583-0382.

John Reardon

is the father of three children
and has been in public education for 35 years.
He has been a frequent guest on radio and
television programs where his parenting

concepts remain a favorite topic of audiences.

This book is available in bulk quantities.
Place orders through

Glacier Publishing

40 Oak Street
Southington, Connecticut 06489
(860) 621-7644